A note for those with depression

Before delving into the pages of this book, I want to extend a heartfelt message to those who are currently grappling with the weight of depression. I understand the immense challenge of attempting to uplift yourself when trapped in the clutches of negativity. Even the simple act of engaging with this book might seem like an insurmountable task. In light of this, I propose a gentle approach: consider reading just two pages each day, allowing yourself the space to absorb the content at your own pace. Remember, acknowledging your progress, no matter how small, is an essential form of self-compassion that we often overlook as adults. There's no urgency, no pressure – the book will patiently await your return. Above all, I urge you to reach out for support. A doctor would be ideal, but if that isn't feasible, lean on a family member or friend who cares about your well-being. Taking that step to connect is the first stride toward healing. Here's to your mental well-being.

Fame isn't relevant	6
Mollie the Collie	10
Mollies First year	22
The Demics	26
Photography	32
Covid-19	38
Three funerals	48
Depression? Not me	56
Therapy	62
Asking for help	70
Do more of what you love	76
Dog photography	88
Feeling better	130
Other work	138
Coping mechanisms	172
Setting yourself up to win	178
Dealing with panic attacks	186
Social media	190
Some things I have learnt	196
Closing	210
Acknowledgements	214

Fame isn't relevant

In an era where it seems like a new celebrity emerges every five minutes, each with a life story that reads like a Hollywood screenplay – tales of overcoming insurmountable odds, battling through war zones, conquering addiction, and achieving remarkable feats against all odds – I find myself standing apart, humbly acknowledging that my story doesn't fit that grand narrative. My journey has been one of the everyday struggles that countless people around the world silently face. This book is not about making headlines or becoming an overnight sensation. It's about sharing my personal account of navigating the maze of depression and anxiety, two foes that seemingly appeared out of nowhere. It's a reflection on the signs I could have spotted, the individuals who offered their unwavering support, the coping strategies that gradually took shape, and the lessons learned along the way.

I've often marvelled at the parade of inspiring life stories that grace the covers of glossy biographies – tales of heroism that often defy belief. But I've come to realise that my own story, while lacking the grandiosity of Hollywood melodrama, is a story that many people can relate to. It's the story of an ordinary individual, someone who has faced their share of hardships, uncertainties, and internal battles. It's a narrative that doesn't involve conquering mountains or defying gravity, but rather one that revolves around embracing the everyday triumphs and challenges of a life that might not make headlines, but still matters deeply.

In the pages that follow, I share my journey through the lens of a normal (ish) bloke who encountered a rough patch in life, just like millions of others out there. This isn't a tale of excessive drama or over-the-top inspiration. Instead, it's a candid account of how I found a way to navigate the stormy waters of mental health challenges and emerge on the other side. I'll discuss how the simple joys of dog walking and the therapeutic power of photography were the lifelines that kept me grounded amidst the storm.

So, if you're looking for an awe-inspiring story of triumph over impossible odds, I'm sorry – this isn't that kind of book. But if you're seeking a relatable narrative of a regular person who faced down his demons and discovered how to survive in the process, then I hope this story finds resonance with you. After all, it's the everyday tales that often contain the most genuine and profound lessons, reminding us that strength is not always found in soaring above the clouds, but in the courage to weather the storms that life brings our way.

Mollie the Collie

The day I finally welcomed Mollie into my life was a significant moment. It was a long-awaited decision that had been brewing for years. As a child, I had yearned for a dog, but my mum's practicality and preference for cats always swayed our household towards feline friends. Turning 30 marked a turning point, and the time felt right to fulfil a dream I had nurtured since childhood.

I've never been one to dawdle when it comes to decisions. Some might say I lean towards impulsivity, but when I set my mind on something, I tend to act swiftly. One day, a realisation struck me like a bolt of lightning – I needed purpose, a reason to wake up with enthusiasm every morning, a companion to share my adventures and keep me on my toes. That moment of clarity propelled me forward.

Looking back, it seemed like fate had conspired to lead me to Mollie, my four-legged partner in crime. The anticipation had been building for years, and when the opportunity finally presented itself, I seized it without hesitation.

Before I bought her I sought guidance from my uncle Dominic, who had a good bit of experience with dogs. He had a couple of noteworthy four-legged friends in his life, like Bullseye and Kabaddi. Bullseye was a stand-out memory. Back when I was a kid, she was part of our family – a pit bull with a fierce demeanour that I can still recall vividly. Despite her tough exterior, she had a heart of gold when it came to my uncle. Their bond was unbreakable, a testament to the loyalty that dogs show to their humans.

Dominic's living situation at one point led to him moving in with my grandma. It was during this time that Bullseye's story took an unexpected turn. Alongside my grandma's big, fluffy cat, Seamus, the household dynamics shifted. Seamus seemed to take joy in taunting Bullseye, asserting his feline dominance. He knew Bullseye wasn't allowed to 'go for him' and he revelled in that knowledge. It's still a chuckle-worthy memory – my uncle once said something along the lines of "You've broken my dog." This being because grandma's touch had transformed Bullseye from a spirited pit bull into a pampered pooch, cuddled up in cosy comfort. It was a shift from fierce protector to a content and pampered pup, proving that even the toughest of dogs can have their hearts won over by love and warmth.

A couple of memories involving Dominic and Bullseye remain etched in my mind. I recall Dominic uttering the words "get him" to Bullseye, which, to my innocent ears, sounded like a command to chase me. And chase me, she did – like a whirlwind, around the table in circles. It was like a scene right out of a Laurel and Hardy sketch. Dominic's laughter filled the room as he said "She's only chasing you because you're running", to which I shouted, "I'm only running because she's chasing me!" Those fleeting seconds felt like an eternity in my young mind, and the memory still brings a smile to my face. Another memory that stands out is a birthday celebration that took an unexpected turn. We decided to go bowling, leaving Bullseye at home alone for a while. My grandma, always trying to be prepared, had set the table with my birthday cake placed perfectly in the centre, ready for our return. On our return there was a single paw print in the cake, right in the middle. The sight of that paw print was initially a shock, and I might have shed a tear or two, something that is embarrassing to admit. But thankfully, no harm was done. She hadn't indulged in the cake itself; instead, she had contentedly licked the frosting off her paw. It was a moment that captured Bullseye's playful spirit and left us with a story to cherish, even if it did involve a slightly altered birthday cake.

After Bullseye's time came to an end, Dominic couldn't bear the emptiness that followed. So, he welcomed another dog into his life – Kabaddi. This new addition was a mix of various breeds, a concoction that somehow embodied the quintessential dog that kids would sketch when asked to draw one. Kabaddi had an appearance that could melt hearts, a true gentle giant. In my eyes, she seemed like the kind of dog who could bring smiles to anyone who crossed her path. Kabaddi's presence was a warm, comforting one. She was that companion who never left Dominic's side, a loyal companion who trotted alongside him wherever he ventured. I remember hearing tales of her off-leash adventures, following him with unwavering devotion. There were stories of how she'd wait patiently outside shops while Dominic ran errands, a testament to her trust in him. It wasn't a practice I necessarily endorsed, but it was undoubtedly a remarkable display of their bond – the kind of connection that transcends words and leashes.

I also reached out for advice from my other uncle, John Paul, or JP as we call him, along with his wife Jan. They've had a bunch of dogs over the years and even got involved in competitions with them. A funny memory I have of them involves a time when my grandma and I decided to visit their house to break up the dogs' day a bit. JP and Jan uncharacteristically had to be out most of the day. It was kind of a new thing for us, and I was still a bit wary of dogs, being a kid and all. The dogs knew us and were friendly enough, but after a while, both my grandma and I started feeling like one of the dogs was eyeing us a bit too intently. We pretty much bolted out of there, like we were fleeing for our lives. When JP and Jan got back home and saw that my grandma had left her handbag behind, they found it hilarious. To them, their dogs were harmless, so they couldn't understand our reaction. It was a funny reminder of how people's perceptions of dogs can be so different.

Back to Mollie, JP and Jan had given me a pretty extensive list of places to steer clear of when it came to getting a dog. They were all about avoiding places associated with puppy farming or having a bad reputation. Dominic, being the resourceful guy he was, had initially lined up a viewing with someone he knew, but for some reason, that plan fell apart. I could tell he was frustrated by it – I guess he wanted to come through for me. But days turned into weeks, and my eagerness got the best of me. I started browsing online, looking at various places, and eventually stumbled upon one in Swinton, if I remember correctly. That's when I decided to hop on my motorbike and head over there to check things out.

Arriving at the place, I was honestly taken aback. It was quite impressive. A large pet store was right there, and the puppy section was attached to it in a separate building.

As I walked in, I found myself in a long corridor. It was lined with glass doors on either side, each leading to a kennel. Inside each kennel, there was fresh hay and water bowls. The sight was a colourful assortment of different breeds – Dalmatians, German Shepherds, Boxers, French Bulldogs – you name it. It felt like they had about twenty different breeds on display. And what caught my eye were the pictures hanging on the walls – snapshots of celebrities holding these very puppies. I have to admit, the whole setup seemed quite legitimate to me.

And then, there were the Collies – the breed I had my heart set on. Intelligent, brimming with energy – exactly what I was seeking. The kennel was labelled "Red Merle Border Collies". These pups were a lively bunch, a fur ball of chaos as they clambered over one another, their energy amusing. Every one of them was already spoken for, except for one. Mollie, though she didn't have a name yet. Amidst the exuberant chaos, she stood apart, displaying a certain solemnity. It was almost as if she knew she was the last pick, the last option.

For those considering getting a puppy, here's a tip: don't lift them until you're certain. There's something about that moment of contact that forms an instant connection, like an invisible bond between you two.

The moment I scooped her up, my heart melted without a trace of embarrassment. The connection was instantaneous. I was looking at a fee of around £350, with a £50 deposit. Without a second thought, I handed over that deposit on the spot. I then hopped on my motorbike and raced back home, where I immediately phoned my sister, urging her to accompany me back. As we returned to the kennel, I could tell Mollie was a bit nervous, her body language giving it away. It was a quality I didn't truly contemplate at the time, but all I wanted was to comfort and reassure her. And so, we brought her home, armed with around £100 worth of bedding, toys, food, treats, leashes, and harnesses – everything a young pup could possibly need.

In due time, she settled down, curling up in her bed after what must have been an exhausting day for her. The following weeks were a whirlwind of toilet training efforts and the search for the perfect name. I cycled through countless options, each one falling short of capturing her essence.

It was during a Harry Potter movie marathon that a scene caught my attention – Arthur Weasley calling out for his wife, Molly. It struck me then – the simplest, most common name for a Collie, sod it I'll just go with that. And so, Mollie the Collie became her name, the spelling 'i.e.' instead of 'y', a small distinction I made simply because.

MOLLIE COLLIE

During those initial days, Mollie had a definite fondness for cozying up next to me. While I was engrossed in working on my laptop, she skillfully made her way up my leg and onto the table, seeking some affectionate moments.

Mollie's first year

In Mollie's first year, things were a real mix of ups and downs. I called her "bipolar Mollie" because her moods would swing like a pendulum from happy to moody in no time. I did my best – signed her up for puppy classes, took her for long walks, and trained her diligently – but those sudden shifts in mood were just part of who she was. Sometimes, they'd come out of nowhere. Like in the morning, she'd be all playful with my feet, but come the afternoon after a nice walk, if I moved my feet on the sofa, she'd snarl and look away. Training her had its quirks too. She got recall, sit, and paw down without a hitch – like she was born knowing them. But when it came to "paw," things could get interesting. She'd raise her paw for a handshake just like we practiced, but every now and then, when she'd had enough, she'd turn her head away and give a little lip curl. It was like she had her own unique way of understanding these commands, making our journey together that much more unpredictable.

Seeking a solution, I sought advice from friends and family, eagerly trying out every suggestion they offered. Yet, despite my commitment to following their advice, Mollie's behaviour remained steadfast. I even paid a visit to the vet in search of guidance, only to be met with a lack of answers and a referral to a behaviourist.

While I can't recall the exact cost of these behaviourist visits, I do remember they were absurdly expensive, far beyond what I could afford. I explored countless avenues – tuning in to television shows, burying myself in books, changing up routines, experimenting with different meals – but nothing seemed to make a dent in her unpredictable moods. The happiness she brought me during her cheerful moments was consistently counteracted by these sudden downturns in her temperament. During one outing, I joined my Uncle JP and Auntie Jan as they engaged in dog training with their own pack. In a well-intentioned effort, JP attempted to assist with Mollie's training, only to experience a nip from her. It was a minor incident, but I felt a mixture of distress and embarrassment. JP brushed it off with his usual humour, yet my unease lingered. Several weeks elapsed, and when my grandmother's sister came to visit, an incident further exacerbated my concerns. I happened to be out of the room when she tried to pet Mollie. In hindsight, Mollie was cornered as a hand reached out for a stroke, which likely contributed to her reaction. Though I believed the bite was driven by fear rather than aggression, the episode left me deeply ashamed and profoundly troubled. Worries gnawed at me: I had two young nieces – what if I wasn't present, and Mollie acted out again? The thought was overwhelming. Fortunately, my grandma's sister brushed off the incident, urging me not to dwell on it.

And thus, the heart-wrenching contemplation of parting ways with Mollie emerged after about a year. With a heavy heart, I dialled the number for the Dogs Trust, my tears flowing even before the call connected. As I spoke to them, I inquired about their re-homing process, seeking to understand how it operated and whether my opinion would carry any weight. In my eyes, Mollie required someone with an abundance of time, patience, and crucially, experience. While I gleaned the necessary information from the call, I needed time to mull over this decision. It brought to mind a television program I had watched, where mothers continued to love their sons despite their heinous actions. Mollie wasn't that bad of course, but I loved her despite the stress she was causing me.

Returning to square one, I resolved to offer Mollie more time and focus. I extended our walks, twice a day, providing her with an outlet for her energy. Whenever she exhibited good behaviour, I made a point to reward her. Establishing a consistent routine became essential, and I communicated to my family the importance of letting her approach them on her own terms. Mollie had developed an uncanny knack for signalling when she wanted attention – a burst of enthusiasm that lasted a mere minute before she'd retreat and find a cosy spot to rest. It was in these instances that I often quipped, "Let sleeping dogs lie."

The Demics

Finding a sense of community in an unexpected place, my path crossed with a tight-knit group of friends who shared the daily ritual of walking their dogs in our local park. Each of them was a seasoned dog owner, with a trove of experiences to share. Our chance encounters evolved into more frequent meetings over a span of weeks. Mollie, still in the early stages of her journey at barely a year old, wielded her puppy charm with finesse, and they couldn't help but adore her. What intrigued me most was her interaction with their dogs – a mix of nervousness and curiosity that painted her in a unique light. These chance encounters led to an invitation to join their walks, and eventually, I found myself welcomed into their private Facebook group. Their chosen moniker, "the Demics," was imbued with humour, given that nearly every member bore some sort of hidden ailment or health issue, all of which remained invisible to the naked eye.

Within this unique dog-walking community, I discovered a tapestry of distinct personalities and their canine companions. Sharon, a devoted greyhound lover, shared her life with Budge, a very tall black greyhound, and also dedicated her time to volunteering for a greyhound rescue charity. Sarah was accompanied by Kodi, a bear of a dog in my eyes. A huge and fluffy northern Inuit that had a past filled with quirks that he seemed to have outgrown in my eyes, embracing a sweet disposition that even allowed him to tolerate Mollie's playful teasing. Gaynor and Boris added their own dynamic energy to the mix. Boris, a spirited Jack Russell, was a stand-out example of well-honed training among Jack Russell's, a breed known for its high energy and determination. Then Nikki and Tracey, two hilarious women, who walked alongside Tikaani another northern Inuit like Kodi. Despite Tikaani's imposing appearance and vocal nature, a gentle and affectionate heart beat beneath his formidable exterior. There was Sam who was accompanied by Teddy and Poppy, two greyhounds with contrasting personalities. Teddy, more reserved perhaps due to past experiences, wore a muzzle around certain dogs and tended to linger at the back patiently waiting for a treat now and again. Poppy radiated a lively energy that could spark in any direction and loved a mad chaotic dash around the fields. Anthony had Ruby alongside him, a chocolate coloured Labrador who was as friendly as they come. Although slowing down when I joined the group due to her age, she still got around and loved to swim. Then we had Jude, an elderly lady, occasionally joined us with Pi, her Shih Tzu companion, and in time Natalie and her diva-like Husky, Misty, became part of our group. Misty had an uncanny knack for luring Natalie into complacency before dashing off into the forest, vanishing for hours. Each dog bore its own distinct temperament, a living testament to the fact that the adage about dogs being all the same couldn't be further from the truth.

Sharon, Sarah, and Gaynor became invaluable sources of guidance during those initial encounters on the park. Their wisdom spanned from walking techniques to deciphering Mollie's body language, and even dietary recommendations. An eye-opening realisation emerged: frequently, it's the owner's behaviour that requires adjusting, rather than the dog's. Their advice, coupled with our shared camaraderie, led to a playful name for themselves as my "demic mums." While Mollie's quirky mood swings didn't entirely disappear, she did show marked improvement, thriving in the daily companionship of our newfound pack.

As time passed, I had the chance to meet everyone's significant others. Whether it was through party invitations or joining us on the park, I gradually got to know them. Keith, Dave, Guido, James, and Michelle – they all extended their warm welcome to me. Not once did I feel like an outsider in their midst.

The Demics crew was all about the daily dog walks. Every morning, we'd get notifications on Facebook with the time and meeting spot for the day's adventure. We had a bunch of different spots we rotated through, and since I didn't have a car, someone from the group always picked me up. Some days, we'd mix things up and go farther away than usual, like hitting the beach where our dogs would go nuts on the sand and in the waves.

But those walks were more than just exercise for our pups. They were our chance to connect, swap stories, and laugh with each other. We had our struggles and tough times, but being out there together, we were a tribe. It wasn't just about our dogs; it was about having people who got it, who were dealing with their own stuff. These walks were like therapy sessions in nature.

In those walks, we found more than just a way to tire out our dogs. We found a community, a group of different folks who could support each other and have a laugh. Day after day, season after season, those walks were our constant. And they gave us more than just exercise – they gave us a lifeline, usually filled with laughter. Those walks with the Demics opened my eyes to something fundamental about dog walking. It's not just about clocking miles or minutes; it's about letting your dog and yourself have a blast. We often get caught up in treating it like a chore – a box to tick off our list. But being with this crew made me realise that dog walking is a gift, a joy that should be embraced fully. With the Demics, it wasn't just about getting from point A to point B. It was about being in the moment, letting our dogs explore, play, and simply be dogs. We'd linger, let them sniff around, chase each other, and splash in puddles. And we'd join in too, sharing laughs and stories while our dogs revelled in their freedom. The walks were a reminder that life's not just about rushing through tasks; it's about relishing the experience.

In a world that's often fast-paced and demanding, those walks were a breath of fresh air. They taught me to slow down, savour the present, and appreciate the simple pleasures of life. The Demics showed me that dog walking isn't just about physical exercise – it's about nourishing the soul and forging connections, both with our furry friends and with each other. Ultimately, this experience highlighted the significance of exchanging greetings during my dog walks. I believe this friendly gesture, often associated with Northern English culture, carries substantial value. Engaging in this habit, such as saying "good morning," proved pivotal, as it led me to an unexpected encounter with the Demics. Without embracing this simple act, I might have missed out on forming a valuable connection with new friends.

Photography

Amidst those walks with the Demics, something rekindled within me – my old passion for photography. It was a spark that had first ignited when I was just 18. Back then, I had a friend named Howard, a pal of my mother's who was about 25 years my senior. Despite the age gap, we found common ground in two passions that would leave a lasting imprint on my life: motorcycling and photography.

Howard was all about motorcycles, and his enthusiasm was contagious. Those Sundays we spent together were all about the thrill of the open road, the wind rushing past us, and the harmonious roar of engines beneath us. Words couldn't entirely convey the feeling of freedom I experienced.

But Howard wasn't a one-dimensional biker; he was also a dedicated photographer. He wielded his camera with ease, freezing moments in time with a simple click. His lens would focus on me as I sped by on my motorbike, capturing the essence of that rush. As our friendship grew, he invited me to join him on his photography ventures – from weddings to equestrian events. I got a taste of the world behind the camera, a realm where moments became stories. I saw first-hand how he transformed everyday occurrences into extraordinary snapshots of emotion and life.

However, even though I was immersed in Howard's photographic world, I never felt the desire to take up photography myself. I respected his talent, but I was content to observe from the sidelines.

Howard had a darkroom – a sacred space where time seemed to stand still and the outside world was shut out. In that red-lit realm, the rules of colour bent to the will of the process. Safe lights cast an eerie glow, allowing us to work without ruining the photosensitive paper. It was a domain of muted shadows and serene reflection, permeated by the scent of chemicals hanging in the air. The patience and precision demanded by this craft were truly remarkable. Howard treated each photograph as a delicate masterpiece, well aware that he was preserving memories for generations to come.

Fast-forwarding many years, life delivered a harsh blow: Howard's unexpected passing. I learned about it on the eve of his funeral, and the shock hit me with full force. Attending his service the next day, my emotions were still in disarray. The grief was overwhelming. In that moment of mourning, I realised that Howard's legacy transcended mere memories. He had imparted to me the fragility of existence, the significance of friendship, and the artistry of capturing fleeting moments. His absence stood as a stark reminder of life's brevity and the importance of the connections we form. Howard's influence remained within me, his way of living a testament to embracing life on one's terms. He showed me how to see beauty in everyday things, to cherish each moment, and to appreciate the wonder of capturing life with a camera.

His friendship taught me that life is a mix of adventures and unexpected turns, highlighting the importance of the relationships we build.

And so, amidst the company of the Demics, I began to capture our escapades using my iPhone – snapshots of laughter, nature's splendour, serene landscapes, and, most importantly, our dogs. What I finally comprehended, an aspect that eluded me during my time with Howard, was that photography isn't just about personal joy; it's about spreading joy to others. The smiles and positive feedback from the Demics, inspired by my pictures of their beloved dogs, ignited a newfound passion within me. It was a realisation that through photography, I could not only find personal satisfaction but also bring happiness to those around me. The following year was marked by my dedication to photography, where I immersed myself in capturing moments while keeping a keen watch on the weather to ensure optimal lighting. Admittedly, I was never entirely satisfied with the quality of the shots, given that my iPhone's camera at the time didn't boast the highest capabilities. Nonetheless, I pressed on, recognising that the results were adequate for the present moment.

TWO WHEELS

Captured in this image is myself astride my inaugural motorbike, the Hyosung XRX 125, navigating Rivington Road in Belmont. The shot was taken by Howard, who cheered me on to accelerate and embrace the full power of the throttle.

Covid-19

Then came a curve ball – the Covid-19 pandemic. A period most of us want to forget. I remember my mum's birthday, standing at the end of her driveway, unable to hug due to the rules. My thoughts on the pandemic and it's legitimacy shifted from unsure to convinced and back again, a roller-coaster that doesn't matter now.

Our dog-walking group got messed up. No more big gatherings, just smaller pairs. Sharon and Sam walked together, Sarah often took Tikaani out for Nikki and Tracey, and Natalie and I went on many long dog walks. In England, the pandemic hit when spring was starting, a season with loads of sun that stretched into summer and even autumn. Everyone seemed to be doing up their gardens, and B&Q was taking forever to deliver stuff. I'm convinced that the weather during that initial year of the pandemic was a lifeline that helped us all maintain our sanity.

As if the weight of the pandemic wasn't already enough, another blow came my way. I had to face the consequences of avoiding and suppressing my emotions. The losses of Howard and the complicated feelings surrounding my father's death soon after had been buried deep within me. I had hidden the pain behind getting a dog, (something I didn't realise until therapy years on), and my growing interest in photography. But life has a way of catching up with you.

My dad, Kevin as I will now refer to him, had left before I even entered this world, leaving behind a void that had been a persistent presence in my life. Around the age of 12, I made the decision to meet him, a choice that would eventually lead to bitter-sweet memories and unresolved feelings. My mum knew how to track him down and arranged a meeting. Our interactions during those brief encounters left me feeling like an outsider, a third wheel in the fragile connection we were trying to forge. This sense of unease and inadequacy gnawed at me, shaping my perception of our relationship, regardless of the actual circumstances.

One weekend, circumstances prevented Kevin from having me over – maybe a funeral or some other event. The following weekend, my family asked if I was planning to visit him, but I hesitated. I couldn't bring myself to go without a direct invitation. My grandma brushed off my concerns, telling me to simply show up, but I yearned to feel truly wanted. Sadly, the call never came. Weeks turned into a silent passage of time, and just like that, my father slipped away from my life once more. The fleeting connection I had attempted to rekindle was abruptly severed, leaving me with a sense of emptiness and a gnawing feeling of rejection.

The next time Kevin entered my world was through a phone call from his stepson, Mark. His sombre voice conveyed that Kevin had suffered a massive heart attack, and the doctors were uncertain about how much time he had left. Mark hesitated, unsure if I would want the opportunity to say goodbye or if such a gesture would be too complicated for me. At that moment, I was at work, but my boss immediately urged me to go without needing a full explanation of my inner turmoil. I rushed to the hospital, and as soon as I saw him, tears welled up and spilled uncontrollably. Through my sobs, I asked to know why he never called me over all those years. His response, was a simple "I don't know." We cried together, perhaps sharing the weight of missed opportunities and unspoken emotions. I held his hand tightly for a moment, and eventually, I left the hospital, thinking that perhaps this encounter marked the closing chapter of our story. As fate unfolded, he managed to survive that ordeal, though it was a precarious existence. The following eighteen months, if I recall correctly, saw him tethered to an array of machines—about half of that time was spent in the hospital, and the other half at home. Surgical intervention wasn't possible due to his condition, leaving him in a state of limbo as medical professionals waited to see if his condition would improve enough for a potential operation. That improvement never materialised, and eventually, he passed away. I remember my first thought was I had seen Kevin less than ten times in my life, and I could count that on two hands.

During those months, I visited him at his home on three or four occasions, each visit lasting around an hour. It seemed like the right thing to do, but our conversations were sparse. His fatigue and illness made it difficult for us to engage in more in-depth discussions. He inquired about my job, my family (which he had once been a part of), and we exchanged the obligatory British small talk about the weather. The interactions were punctuated by a sense of awkwardness, a reflection of the complex emotions that lay beneath the surface.

At the funeral, I positioned myself near the back of the church, seeking solace in the presence of my sister (whom we shared the same mum, different dad's), who had kindly offered to accompany me to offer her emotional support. As people began to piece together my identity, I could feel their curious glances directed my way. The eulogies reverberated through the sacred space, recounting his life in glowing terms. They praised his devotion as a son, a father, a husband – a caring and affectionate presence in the lives of his entire family. Grandchildren were mentioned, love was extolled, yet my existence remained absent from the narrative. Amidst the heartfelt reminiscences, I held out hope for a letter, a photograph, a cherished token that he might have left for me, something that acknowledged our lost history. Alas, there was nothing.

At the subsequent wake, I had the chance to meet my granddad and aunt. Their demeanour was warm and welcoming, expressing a genuine desire to bridge the gap that had long existed. We met over the course of several occasions, sharing pub lunches and coffee outings. Yet, despite these interactions, a palpable sense of otherness lingered. A birthday card, a Christmas card – they arrived in due course, but each one seemed to carry an unspoken distance. The past was left unspoken, an enigma that I struggled to decipher. Gradually, the cards and texts dwindled, the connection fading as swiftly as it had come.

Consequently, I found myself grappling with a sense of dismissal, fostering the belief that their unwillingness to engage was ultimately their forfeiture. The divide that had endured among us had widened so much that I might as well have been a stranger, despite our shared family connection. The loss of two influential individuals—one who held the potential for significance, but never realised it, and the other a cherished companion—appeared to exert a considerable weight upon my thoughts. The burden weighed on my subconscious, eventually reaching a pinnacle in an unexpected manner.

And so, amidst the backdrop of the pandemic, my life took an unexpected turn with my first panic attack. In the quiet hours of around 3 a.m., I awoke to the sensation of an invisible weight pressing heavily on my chest. In my groggy state, irrational thoughts of the supernatural initially crossed my mind – a reaction borne out of fear and disorientation. As reality set in, it dawned on me that this could be a medical issue. Gathering my resolve, I made my way to the hospital, plagued by lingering chest discomfort. Once there, the hospital staff engaged in a battery of tests – electrodes, blood draws – all of which ultimately yielded the reassurance that physically, I was fine. Yet, the perplexing nature of my experience persisted.

A compassionate nurse asked a question that touched on my emotional state, "Is there anything significant happening in your life right now? Any major changes or stressors?" A flood of recent events cascaded from me: the loss of Howard, my almost stranger of a biological father passing away, his family's tentative outreach, a recent breakup, and the relentless demands of work. With empathy, the nurse illuminated the possibility that the emotional weight I had carried, coupled with a lack of outlets, could have manifested in the form of a panic attack.

She emphasised the importance of finding someone to confide in, someone who could lend an ear and share the burden. It wasn't about finding solutions, but about releasing the pressure valve on my pent-up emotions. Her question resonated deeply, exposing the absence of a trusted confidant in my life. The revelation served as a stark reminder that bottling up feelings could trigger a cascade of mental and physical turmoil.

Over the next few months I had many panic attacks, some worse than others. What is horrible about panic attacks is they can manifest out of nowhere, at any time. You can't prepare for them, and they leave you pretty much immobile in discomfort. I found myself diving into self-education as a last resort. I became a student of my own experiences, seeking out information and trying to comprehend the intricate workings of my mind during those challenging moments. I embarked on a journey to understand panic attacks better, to decode the triggers and unravel the mechanics that set them in motion. I devoured articles, books, and online resources, hoping to find some clarity amidst the chaos. It was a strange sensation, studying my own panic attacks from a distance, as if I were observing a puzzle slowly assembling itself.

I tried out different mindfulness apps and exercises to find some peace. Funny thing, some of these methods meant to help actually made my panic attacks worse. It felt like adding fuel to the fire. Each time I failed, I learned that there's no one-size-fits-all fix for panic attacks – they're as different as the people who go through them.

After some trial and error, I stumbled onto something that clicked for me. I noticed my panic attacks pretty much lasted an hour each time. Armed with this realisation, I started a bit of an odd routine. When I felt panic creeping in, I'd find a quiet spot, note the time, and tell myself that I was about to face an hour of discomfort. I'd remind myself that even though it felt uncomfortable, it wasn't medically harmful and couldn't really hurt me. It was my way of facing the clock, committing to get through the storm. I also found an unexpected lifeline my mum's voice. When panic got too overwhelming, I'd call her and put the phone on speaker while lying on the floor. I'd ask her to chat or tell stories. Her voice, a reassuring presence, helped ease the tension.

What my journey showed me is that panic is personal. We all deal with it our own way. There's no one-size-fits-all solution, no magic trick. It's about trying different things, finding what clicks for us, and creating our own strategies to cope.

With time and persistence, the panic attacks started to fade in frequency and intensity. They didn't vanish overnight, but I slowly got a grip.

Three funerals

Just as I was starting to figure out how to get to grips with panic attacks, we as a family got the news of my uncle Vance's passing. He had been fighting cancer for a while, a battle he couldn't win in the end. My relationship with Vance was a mix of arguments and camaraderie. His love for a drink often led to heated discussions, and our differing viewpoints were clear. Yet, despite our clashes, he was family. And family meant more to me than our disagreements.

Vance's passing brought to light the fact that unresolved conflicts and suppressed emotions can resurface unexpectedly. I was upset on behalf of my grandma and mother, as well as my cousin Aimee, who had travelled from New Zealand to see him in his final days along with her mother, only to return home knowing she would probably never see him again. Feeling the ache of missed opportunities and the sadness of his absence, it served as a stark reminder that life's challenges continue alongside your personal journey of growth and healing, pushing you to confront both the past and the present in ways you might not have anticipated.

Vance's passing was yet another twist in the unpredictable road of life, serving as a powerful reminder that our journeys are never straightforward. The path is filled with unexpected bends, unforeseen encounters, and moments that catch us off guard. It taught me the importance of confronting discomfort, addressing unresolved issues, and, most importantly, navigating life's ever-changing terrain with both resilience and compassion.

Amid life's trials, I found myself assuming the role of a sturdy support for my grandmother, mother, and aunt. Their reliance on me, coupled with the praises from them and extended family members for my unwavering strength, provided a glimmer of encouragement. I held back my own sorrow, wearing a brave mask to guide them through the turbulent waters of grief. It was a duty I embraced willingly, driven by a deep commitment to my family's well-being.

Yet, beneath the surface of our familial interactions, another storm was brewing. My uncle Dominic had been quietly battling cancer, shielding the true extent of his struggle from us all. We were aware of his battle with cancer, yet the extent of its severity remained a mystery to us. We assumed that because he had undergone treatment, that the situation was progressing positively.

Dominic was a man of extraordinary compassion, a lover of dogs, a rugged cowboy with a Viking's spirit caught in the wrong era in my opinion. He embodied a sense of effortless coolness, and his presence radiated warmth and laughter.

He had taken it upon himself to shield our grandmother from any further heartache, aware of her difficulty in coming to terms with Vance's loss. The fact that he shouldered his own pain while safeguarding her heart spoke volumes about his character. Dominic was a true exemplar of selflessness, a quality that defined him in the eyes of those who knew him. Very shortly after Vance had passed, Dominic lost his battle too.

As the pandemics grip persisted, we were faced with another layer of sorrow – the restrictions that barred us from attending Dominic's funeral due to Covid limitations. In hindsight, it's a frustrating memory, especially now that we know while many of us couldn't gather to mourn, governments were busy partying and not caring about isolating at all. But at that moment, it deepened the ache of separation, the inability to come together and mourn as a united family.

Losing Dominic just weeks after Vance was like a double punch to the gut. Two beloved family members gone so close together left us stunned and struggling to grasp the reality. It was a stark reminder that life is unpredictable, fragile, and keeps moving no matter what.

During this time, my primary mission became uplifting the spirits of my mother and grandmother. I put my own grief and challenges on hold, inadvertently neglecting my own needs as I poured my energy into supporting them. The weight of their sorrow took precedence over my own, and in my determination to be the pillar of strength they needed, I unintentionally pushed aside my own mourning and unresolved issues.

Looking back, I have no regrets about being there for my mother and grandmother during those challenging times. Their well-being was my priority, and I stand by my choice to support them wholeheartedly. However, hindsight reveals that I could have managed the situation more effectively, finding a balance between being a rock for them and tending to my own emotional needs. It's a lesson learned through experience – the importance of caring for oneself while caring for others, a delicate equilibrium that I continue to navigate.

Time marched on, slipping away as I tried to navigate the turbulence of grief and loss, seeking a semblance of normality in its wake. But just as life tentatively resumed its rhythm, a sudden phone call shattered the fragile balance. My mother's voice trembled as she shared unsettling news – my uncle Zane had disappeared from the scene for days. His friend's struggle to access his apartment fuelled a gnawing unease, hinting at a possibility none of us wanted to entertain. Was it conceivable that he had passed away?

Sitting with my grandmother, a mixture of worry and foreboding settled within me. How could I possibly broach such a heavy topic with her, knowing the immense losses she had already endured? Excusing myself, I stepped outside to field the calls, shielding my grandmother from the conversation unfolding. Each call brought more uncertainty, but a sombre truth was emerging – Zane's absence had taken a permanent and irreversible form.

Tears brimmed in my eyes as I sat outside, the weight of the news crashing down upon me. The world around me blurred as I grappled with the overwhelming reality of another loss. Stumbling through the emotional storm, I tried to steady myself against the unrelenting tide of tragedy. I couldn't bring myself to go back inside and break the news to my grandma. I made calls in a daze of disbelief, unsure of where to turn. My grandmother's sister first, and then my uncle JP—they offered comforting words on the other end.

As I urged my grandma to take a seat and brace herself for what I was about to say, her hands began to tremble. I spoke as softly as I could, breaking the news gently, and in response, she let out a gasp, her whole body quivering. I wrapped my arms around her, feeling my own throat tighten as I struggled to find the right words to offer comfort.

The unity of family in times of hardship was a heartwarming sight to behold. Within minutes around ten family members had shown up. Amidst the tears and shared grief, there was an overwhelming sense of solidarity, a powerful reminder that no one need bear the weight of loss alone. We leaned on each other, finding strength in the connections that bound us. Within minutes, our family's infamous sense of humour kicked in, a coping mechanism we had honed over years of ups and downs. We started sharing stories and fond memories of Zane, swapping anecdotes that brought both laughter and tears. It was remarkable how humour became a refuge, a welcome diversion from the weight of our sorrow. However, as the dust began to settle, a harsh reality stared us in the face—Zane's sudden departure had left behind a financial vacuum. There were no resources to bear the cost of a funeral, a prospect that weighed heavily on our hearts. It was a moment that underscored the profound impact of loss on every level. Swallowing our pride, we eventually turned to a GoFundMe campaign, seeking assistance from friends, family, and even strangers to give Zane a proper farewell. It was a humbling experience, a reminder that in times of adversity, reaching out for help was not a sign of weakness but an acknowledgment of our shared humanity. In this moment, I would like to re-thank everyone who kindly donated during our difficult time, it meant the world to us as a family.

Depression? Not me

During my twenties I would have never anticipated going through depression. As I grew older, my confidence grew too —as a designer, as a person, as a man. So, it's quite surprising as I sit here today, realising that I had spent years dealing with depression without really knowing. But the thing is, men still don't really talk about it, so how are we supposed to recognise the signs? Sure, you might hear a celebrity mention it here and there, and people commend them for their courage. However, the truth is, I didn't recognise I was depressed. And when I finally did, I didn't want to admit it, not to myself, and definitely not to anyone else.

When I took a step back and really contemplated, I started piecing things together. I knew I had gained weight, but I somehow brushed it off as inconsequential. I wasn't enjoying the simple act of dog walking, something that once brought me joy. My temper grew shorter, and I found myself snapping over trivial matters. Afternoons became my refuge for sleep – a refuge from the emotional exhaustion that seemed to grip me. I would get nine hours sleep overnight and wake up feeling tired, and mundane tasks like having a shower took all my energy. It was only when I finally accepted that depression had a hold on me that I began to see the puzzle coming together. It's funny how we can be so blind to the most obvious things when we're stuck in the midst of it all.

It was my mum who suggested depression, having been through it herself. Once I opened my eyes to the possibility of depression, the signs were glaringly evident. It was like uncovering a hidden layer of my reality. It wasn't just about feeling sad; it was the accumulation of all these subtle changes that had slipped under my radar. I could clearly feel the disconnect between what I did and how I felt. It's strange how the mind can trick us into believing that everything is just fine when it's not.

Depression had become a part of my life, silently weaving its threads into my daily experiences. Panic attacks were the sparks that ignited the fire, and the ensuing months painted a picture of melancholy that I hadn't seen coming.

I had journeyed from not realising the connection between my weight gain and depression to recognising that my enthusiasm had waned, my temperament was off-kilter, and my afternoons were swallowed by fatigue. Depression had become an undeniable presence, and it was time to confront it head-on I thought. But again, I didn't reach out for help, instead thinking as I had realised I might have depression it would now somehow magically go away.

The turning point in my journey arrived at a time when various elements of my life collided in a disorienting way. It all began with my foray into a new work-from-home job. The initial training sessions were a bit of a blow to my self-esteem, making me feel like a novice despite my experience. The extensive Zoom calls, which had been a staple of the training, entered a new phase around the fifth day. It was time for us to practically apply what we had learned, but the situation quickly spiralled into chaos. The call resembled a verbal battleground, with trainees shouting over each other and the trainer struggling to assert control. Frustration mounted, and I sensed the gradual build-up of a panic attack.

Attempting to keep my cool, I desperately fought against the rising tide of anxiety. But then, like a pressure cooker reaching its limit, I snapped. In an uncharacteristic display of emotion, I slammed my laptop onto the floor and unleashed a string of profanities that reflected my immense irritation. The incident must have been unsettling to my grandmother, who came rushing in to find me sprawled on the floor, my eyes teary and my chest clenched in an agonising grip. It marked one of the most severe panic attacks I had ever experienced, rendering me physically and emotionally shaken for hours on end.

Reflecting on that frightening episode, I was prompted to take action. I realised that my mental health had reached a critical juncture, a point at which I could no longer evade the underlying issues that had been festering within me. It was an abrupt wake-up call, starkly underscoring the fact that I could no longer suppress the emotional turmoil that had been building up over time. The subsequent conversation with the agency that had facilitated my employment became a turning point They connected me with a mental health worker who had a conversation with me for about an hour. She remained composed, letting the conversation flow naturally, asking a series of questions and giving me space to answer at my own pace. Eventually, she recommended seeking assistance and sought my consent to refer me to a counselling service for talking therapy. I gladly accepted.

Therapy

And so, I finally took the plunge and began my therapy sessions. It was talking therapy, they said. I waited for several weeks before I actually walked into that room for the first time, a sign of the backlog and just how many people are waiting for help. It was like a mix of nervousness and a tiny bit of excitement. I wanted to see if this could really help me. The first session, I'll be honest, felt kind of weird. The therapist was this young woman, probably around 23 years old. And I remember thinking, what does she know? How can she understand my life experiences? But I tried to keep an open mind, even though part of me doubted it would make any difference. When the day of the first session arrived, I stepped into the room with a bunch of emotions swirling inside me. It was like a mix of anxiety and maybe a little bit of hope. The therapist sat there, and I just started talking. I told her about everything – my uncles, my dad, and Howard passing away. I felt a little weird just spilling out my life story to a stranger, but I wanted to give it a shot. I talked and talked, trying to cram in all the feelings and experiences that had been weighing on me. By the time I had finished, the session was over, like those scenes in movies where something important happens and then it's suddenly cut off.

At that point, I wasn't sure what to think. The therapist had asked some questions, and I had answered, but it felt like we barely scratched the surface. I left the room feeling a bit puzzled. Was this really going to help? I couldn't help but wonder if it was worth it. But there was also this tiny sense of curiosity – maybe there was something to this whole therapy thing after all.

The following week, I walked into the session with a slightly different mindset. I figured I should give the therapist more of a chance to talk, to guide the conversation. She started asking questions, and we began to go back and forth. This time, I wanted to see where she was taking the conversation.

The first thing we delved into was the fact that I had bottled up so much – five deaths, to be exact. I hadn't really allowed myself to grieve properly for any of them. I had been there as a support system for my family, but I had brushed aside the nurse's advice from that first panic attack. I had kept all those emotions hidden, not really dealing with them. As we talked more, it became clear that I was still doing the same thing – bottling up my feelings instead of facing them. In the following sessions, we went even deeper. We explored unresolved memories from my childhood, relationships that had left their mark on me, and the life choices I had made along the way. It felt like Pandora's box had been opened, and I couldn't believe how much was pouring out. It was like there was a backlog of emotions and experiences that I had never really confronted. It was overwhelming at times, but also strangely liberating. Talking about all these things was like lifting a weight off my shoulders, and for the first time, I started to see how much of an impact they had on my mental health.

Throughout our sessions, the therapist offered me various suggestions each week – try this approach, be mindful of certain things, experiment with new ways of thinking. At the beginning, I must admit, I approached it with a sort of school project mentality. I wanted to demonstrate signs of improvement every week, almost like earning grades. But she reminded me that while it's great to apply what we discussed, I shouldn't put unnecessary pressure on myself. She emphasised that this healing process is gradual and that I shouldn't force myself to "get better" quickly.

One thing she consistently emphasised was that the work was being done by me. She was there to guide, listen, and provide insights, but the real change was coming from within me. As I tried to allow her to dictate the conversation, she would remind me that therapy is about me talking and her listening. Yes she offers advice but to get a good grasp of all I was going through, first I had to open up. And open up I did, finding myself bringing up things from childhood I had forgotten.

It's almost humorous how within the confines of those four walls, with an uninvolved stranger, I found the space and safety to let go of so much. It's as though the environment created the perfect conditions for me to unravel my thoughts and emotions, leading to a newfound clarity and understanding of myself.

Over the course of ten sessions, I delved into some of the deep-rooted issues that I had either forgotten or intentionally pushed aside. My therapist shed light on the concept that our brains are adept at compartmentalising things – locking away experiences in a mental vault to protect us from emotions we may not be prepared to process at the time. However, as time passes, that vault becomes heavier with the weight of unresolved emotions, until it eventually bursts open, demanding our attention. I did my best to apply the strategies and insights she shared, but perhaps the most comforting words she offered were, "We might never fully recover from these experiences, but we can become more skilled at managing the situations and recognising the warning signs, so they don't become as overwhelming in the future." It was a sobering realisation that healing doesn't necessarily mean erasing the pain entirely, but rather finding ways to navigate life with a heightened sense of self-awareness and emotional resilience.

After the conclusion of those ten sessions, I expressed my heartfelt gratitude to my therapist for all the guidance and support she had provided. While I knew I hadn't achieved complete healing in that time, I felt equipped with valuable tools to confront and manage my challenges. Despite this newfound awareness, I still experienced the ebb and flow of the roller-coaster of emotions. There were days when depression would hit me like a freight train, leaving me weighed down and despondent.

I had always cherished New Year's Day as a fresh start, a chance to establish new habits, set fresh goals, and venture into unexplored territories. However, this particular New Year's Day, I awoke under the weight of an immense heaviness that seemed to encompass my entire body. It's crucial to note that I wasn't contemplating suicide, but rather questioning the purpose of my existence. In that moment, I made a difficult decision to reach out to the Samaritans, unsure if it was the right thing to do. Even during my darkest times, I didn't want to burden my friends or family with my inner struggles. Speaking with the Samaritans was a lifeline. They reassured me that reaching out before things become truly dire is exactly what they encourage. They explained that waiting until someone is actively suicidal is considered too late. They shared stories of their own volunteers who reach out for support when they're struggling. It was eye-opening to realise that even those who provide help need help themselves at times, and I should feel no shame in seeking assistance. They suggested considering medication and discussing it with my doctor, but I was hesitant. I didn't want to numb myself to the emotional pain; I wanted to confront and understand the root causes. The important thing is they listened when I needed someone to.

Asking for help

Asking for help when depression was lurking around felt like I was stepping into a maze blindfolded. It wasn't just a matter of reaching out – it was a journey of uncertainty, a road filled with doubts and fears. It meant admitting that I couldn't handle it all on my own, that I needed a lifeline to guide me through the darkness. Looking back, I see now that it was one of the smartest moves I made, even though it wasn't easy.

I remember the first time I let someone in on what I was going through. It felt like standing on the edge of a precipice, unsure if I'd fall or be caught. Opening up to a friend about the battles I was fighting internally wasn't a cure-all, but it was a relief. It felt like I wasn't hiding anymore, like I was letting them into my world, even if just a little. It showed me that maybe I didn't have to carry this weight alone.

Talking to family was much easier. They listened without judgment and had been through similar situations and could relate and offer advice. Sharing the pain that I'd been bottling up was tough, but it was like a weight lifted off my shoulders. It was as if I was acknowledging that I didn't have to be the strong one all the time.

But asking for help wasn't just about words – it was about actions too. I started letting friends know when I wasn't up for social stuff. It felt weird at first, like admitting I couldn't keep up with the norm. But they were surprisingly cool about it. They understood that sometimes I needed space, and that made me feel less guilty about needing that space.

Sure, there were moments when asking for help felt like a confession of weakness. But as time went on, I started to see it as a badge of strength. It wasn't about admitting defeat; it was about taking charge of my own well-being. It wasn't about trying to be a superhero; it was about embracing my humanity. We're not meant to navigate life's struggles alone – we're meant to lean on each other, to find support in our connections.

Dealing with depression was like wrestling with shadows, and I realised I had some habits that I'd fall back on during my lowest moments. One of those habits was diving into junk food. There was a sort of comfort in the crunch of crisps or the chocolate I so craved– a fleeting escape from the turmoil inside. It felt good for a moment, but it never really fixed anything. It was like putting a Band-Aid on a wound that needed stitches.

Chocolate, my one guilty pleasure in a world where I rarely drank alcohol, didn't smoke or dabble in drugs, was my little escape. Giving it up was out of the question. But I started to realise that while it felt good in the moment, it wasn't really helping me manage my emotions. It was like a quick fix that never lasted.

Another habit that came back now and again was the urge to take afternoon naps. Somehow, sinking into sleep during the daylight hours felt like a way to escape the heaviness in my mind. But when I woke up, the heaviness was still there, maybe even stronger. It was like hitting pause on my problems, only to find them waiting for me when I hit play again.

What struck me was how these habits were all about instant gratification. They offered a quick shot of relief, but they never dug into the root issues. It was like trying to fill a hole with sand – sure, it covered it up for a bit, but it didn't really address the gap underneath.

Trying to manage my sweet tooth became a challenge. I didn't want to give up chocolate, but I also didn't want it to be my crutch. It was like finding the balance between enjoying something I loved and not using it as a way to avoid facing my feelings. It wasn't about denying myself happiness, but about finding healthier ways to cope.

In the end, I learned that recognising these habits was a step toward understanding myself better. They were like signposts pointing to the areas where I needed to work on my coping mechanisms. It wasn't about completely cutting out things that brought me joy; it was about reshaping how I approached them. So, if you're in the same boat, struggling with habits that offer a quick escape from your emotions, remember this: it's okay to enjoy the little things, but don't let them be your only way of dealing with the tough stuff. It's about finding healthier ways to navigate the rough waters, and sometimes that means rethinking the role of those instant gratifications in your life. It's a journey of balance and self-discovery, one step at a time.

When I mention that I asked for help, it wasn't me openly declaring, "Hey, I need help!" It was more about sharing with those around me that I was going through a difficult period, that I was battling depression. In a way, I was indirectly asking for understanding, and that, in itself, was a form of seeking help. I recognised that I had a tendency to let my thoughts spiral out of control, overthinking situations, and imagining the worst-case scenarios – like what people might be saying about me behind my back.

I started to communicate my needs to others – expressing when I didn't feel up to going out for a drink, or asking for a bit of space from my family when I sensed things were becoming overwhelming. True help wasn't just someone sitting beside me, reassuring me that everything would be okay. Help came in the form of those who genuinely offered an ear, a listening presence when I needed it the most. I found this kind of support from more people than I expected. It was surprising to realise how many people were willing to be there for me, to lend an understanding ear.

Something intriguing happened when I decided to open up on social media about my struggles and my determination to overcome them. Many people responded by sharing their own experiences, revealing that they had been through or were currently going through similar challenges. It was eye-opening to see the sheer number of individuals who suffer in silence, dealing with their own battles behind closed doors. This realisation underscored the importance of breaking the stigma around mental health, encouraging open conversations, and showing that we're not alone in our struggles.

Do more of what you love

And so, my journey of healing began – a process that I knew would require change, effort, and commitment. It was like my mind was on board, ready to take on this challenge, but my body sometimes struggled to keep up. My grandma's wise saying often came to mind, "The mind is willing, but the flesh is weak." There were days when I felt a surge of energy and motivation, and then there were days when it seemed like all my energy had evaporated. It was surprising how easily my whole day could be thrown off balance by the slightest thing. I'd wake up with a clear plan, only to have an unexpected visitor or a minor disruption, and suddenly, I'd feel like the entire day was derailed and wasted. Those days, I'd just push through, hoping for a fresh start the next day.

The weather, too, played a role in this process. Living in England, we're no strangers to overcast, grey, drizzly days. While cosy on some occasions, the lack of sunshine could often feel like it was zapping my energy. It's amazing how much our environment can impact our mood and motivation. I learned about seasonal affective disorder (S.A.D), often referred to as the winter blues, that cast a shadow on the lives of those affected by its subtle yet profound influence. As the seasons shift and the days grow shorter, a subset of individuals finds themselves grappling with emotional states that mirror the gloomy weather. The lack of sunlight during the colder months triggers a range of symptoms, including lethargy, low mood, and a diminished sense of well-being. Although never diagnosed, I felt I fitted into this definition, just another thing to bring me down I thought. Despite these challenges, I was determined to push forward and make positive changes. I knew that healing wasn't a linear journey – there would be ups and downs, good days and tough days – but the important thing was to keep moving, even if it was one step at a time.

I remember reading in various entrepreneurial books and watching videos online that said, "Do what you love, and you'll never work a day in your life." But I was stuck wondering, what the heck do I really love? I had things I enjoyed, sure, but love? That felt like another level. So, I spent weeks trying to figure it out. I thought about drawing and painting, stuff I kinda liked, but doing that all day, every day? I couldn't wrap my head around it. But I was determined to give it a shot. So I got myself a cheap digital pen and pad, hooked it up to my Adobe software, and started drawing digital art. And you know what? I actually loved it! It was exciting, and I was immersed into it for a several weeks. Then, I don't know, the buzz wore off, and I was back to feeling lost. I thought, seriously, why is it so hard to find something that clicked and stuck with me?

I decided to give talking therapy another go at this stage. I figured I want to move forward and not slide back into that dark place. So, in those sessions, we dove deep into my struggle to find something that really sparked joy in me. My mind was racing with all these things I liked, mixed with my itch for entrepreneurship and my desire to get a grip on my emotions once more. It was during one of these talks that books came up. I happened to mention this children's book idea I'd been carrying around for a while. My therapist looked at me and asked, "So, why haven't you written it?" I couldn't really come up with a solid excuse – sure, I had time, just not the patience, I told her. Well, that same evening, I pulled out my laptop and started typing away.

And so, my new project kicked off – waving digital art goodbye, I dove head first into my children's book idea. I named it "Millie's First Mobile Phone." The story revolved around a young girl who becomes so engrossed in her new phone on Christmas Day that she misses out on everything happening around her. I was consumed by the process, writing every single day. Some days, I battled writer's block, anxiously waiting for sleep to reset my mind with fresh ideas. Interestingly, I found that sleep truly did bring inspiration.

Though writing was one thing, the illustrations were another challenge. With a discerning eye, I knew I wanted the imagery to match the narrative perfectly. That's where my mum came in – she had a distinctive artistic style that suited the project. We embarked on a collaborative journey, with me sending her chapters to read and her creating illustrations that captured the essence of each section. It was a team effort that spanned around two months. I involved other family members to proofread the book, and I meticulously went over every detail, double and triple checking everything. Then, the formatting for printing had to be tackled, ensuring it was set up correctly.

After all the hard work, I decided to take the self-publishing route using Amazon's platform. It seemed like a more accessible path compared to the potential disappointment of facing publisher rejections or navigating the complex traditional publishing process. Amazon simplified the journey, allowing you to realise your dream with just a few clicks – a far cry from the arduous hoops traditional publishers often put authors through.

The number of copies sold remains a vague memory, probably less than fifty, a modest count compared to the literary giants of the world. However, I found myself unbothered by this seemingly small accomplishment. Writing "Millie's First Mobile Phone" had taught me something far more significant, a lesson intertwined with my ongoing therapy sessions.

Through this process, I came to the realisation that patience was a virtue I needed to cultivate more than anything else. My impatience, my rush to reach the end, to heal, to achieve progress with my mental health, was a recurring theme in my life. Yet, the act of writing the book and navigating its journey served as a gentle reminder of the wisdom embedded in the adage, "Good things come to those who wait." Paradoxically, while my impatience had driven me during the writing process, my patience kept me committed, seeing the project through from inception to completion without compromise.

Collaborating with my mum for the illustrations introduced another layer of patience. I had to wait for her drawings, an opportunity that allowed me to shift my focus onto other endeavours. Amid all these realisations, the most impactful lesson was yet to unfold.

During my ongoing therapy sessions, a recurring topic that emerged was my tendency to feel anxious about others' opinions of me and my habitual inclination to compare myself to others. While my therapist assured me that these feelings were natural, she also pointed out a paradox within me – I ardently embraced the desire to live an unconventional life. I didn't want to follow the traditional narrative of house, kids, vacations, retirement, and eventually passing away. My aspirations leaned towards entrepreneurship, cultivating my own business, regardless of its scale. I craved the autonomy of working for myself.

Yet, my therapist gently posed a question that caught me off guard – if I sought an unconventional lifestyle, why was I inflicting the punishment of comparison upon myself? She pointed out that living differently inherently meant being different from others. Consequently, comparing myself to the conventional path was futile and unnecessary. Her insight seemed glaringly obvious once articulated, a revelation my own mind had concealed from me.

During this period, I was also taking care of my grandmother while working on freelance design projects. Strangely, I felt guilt-ridden about my flexible schedule that allowed me to walk my dog at 10:30 in the morning or leave my house whenever necessary. Many of my acquaintances were confined behind office desks, and here I was, living life differently. I was convinced that to truly embody my unique aspirations, I needed to discard concerns about what others thought of me. The irony wasn't lost on me – most likely, they weren't investing much thought into my actions anyway.

With my therapist's guidance echoing in my mind, I embarked on a personal mantra – every time my thoughts veered toward over thinking and worrying about others' perceptions, I reminded myself, "Who cares what others think? This is your life, not theirs." This affirmation became a powerful tool in redirecting my focus away from external judgments. As the weeks went by, I gradually internalised this perspective, but I can't pinpoint the exact moment when it finally clicked.

Around this juncture, I reached an important realisation. I recognised that while I had numerous interests, there were few, if any, that I loved to engage in 100% of the time. And that's perfectly okay. In fact, this understanding became a catalyst for my next revelation – why not embrace a variety of interests and rotate through them as I pleased? This idea contradicted the notion I had absorbed during my schooling years – the belief that being a "jack of all trades, master of none" was an unfavourable way to navigate life.

However, upon deeper reflection, I challenged this belief. After all, I had dedicated a significant portion of my life to design, marketing, and the print industry. I had become proficient through continuous learning and hands-on experience. Why not extend that philosophy to other domains? Why not explore a multitude of interests? With this shift in mindset, I set off on a new quest – a quest to try new things, to embrace different hobbies and pursuits that piqued my curiosity. The idea of being a multifaceted individual, driven by an array of passions, began to excite me.

With newfound enthusiasm, I delved into exploring various interests that had long piqued my curiosity. One of my first forays was into the world of bike riding, a passion I hadn't pursued in years. Engaging with Sharon, my friend from the Demics, and also a dedicated bike enthusiast. I spoke with Anthony who sold me his mountain bike, at a very reasonable price I'm sure he would want me to say. I accompanied Sharon and occasionally Michelle on numerous bike rides over the following months. These experiences opened my eyes not just to how out of shape I was compared to them, but also to the sheer joy of cycling through scenic landscapes and feeling the wind against my face.

Gardening also captured my attention, and I became deeply engrossed in transforming our garden. Working with a shoestring budget, I tackled projects of all sizes. I erected arbours, crafted gates, and devoted time to nurturing plants from their very seeds. The process of learning which plants harmonised best together, exploring the intricacies of rockeries, and even delving into the world of pond maintenance fascinated me. I found satisfaction even in what others might consider mundane tasks – painting fences, meticulously weeding, and nurturing the garden into a thriving sanctuary. The hands-on experience not only cultivated a green haven but also offered a form of therapeutic respite.

Curious to explore new dietary horizons, I decided to venture into the realm of pescetarianism – a vegetarian diet supplemented with fish. Initially, I embarked on this culinary journey without setting any specific time line, thinking I might barely last a week. Yet, to my surprise, I quickly found myself adapting to the new diet and enjoying it immensely. The positive changes I experienced – both in terms of my palate and my overall well-being – motivated me to continue along this path.

As I embraced the pescetarian lifestyle, I noticed a shift not only in my dietary preferences but also in my physical health. Coupled with my newfound interest in bike riding, the diet played a crucial role in helping me shed some of the excess weight I had accumulated over time. The pounds began to melt away, and as a result, I felt an improvement in my mental health as well. What had started as an experiment to explore different eating habits ended up contributing significantly to my holistic well-being. The initial intention of trying this dietary shift for just one week evolved into an eight-month journey that I couldn't help but feel proud of. In one of my therapy sessions, my therapist highlighted the importance of acknowledging our achievements, even the seemingly small ones, as adults often neglect to reward themselves. I took her advice to heart and celebrated both the success of my eight-month pescatarian diet and the transformation in my body and mindset that accompanied it.

Amidst these changes, I found myself drawn even deeper into the realm of photography. I decided to take my hobby more seriously, transforming it from a casual pastime into a dedicated pursuit. It marked the first time I was actively studying photography techniques, eagerly venturing out each day with the goal of capturing at least one exceptional photograph. And you know what? I discovered that feeling of genuine happiness that had eluded me for months. It was as if photography had woven itself into the very fabric of my being, infusing every shot I took with a sense of purpose and joy. My lens became a window to the world, and I seized the opportunity to capture both stunning landscapes and the charismatic companionship of my friends' dogs. The act of photography was no longer confined to just clicking a button; it had become a journey of exploration, a creative outlet that resonated with my soul. The more I immersed myself in this art form, the more I could feel my affection for it growing. Photography had transitioned from a mere liking to an emerging love, infusing my life with colour and meaning in ways I hadn't anticipated.

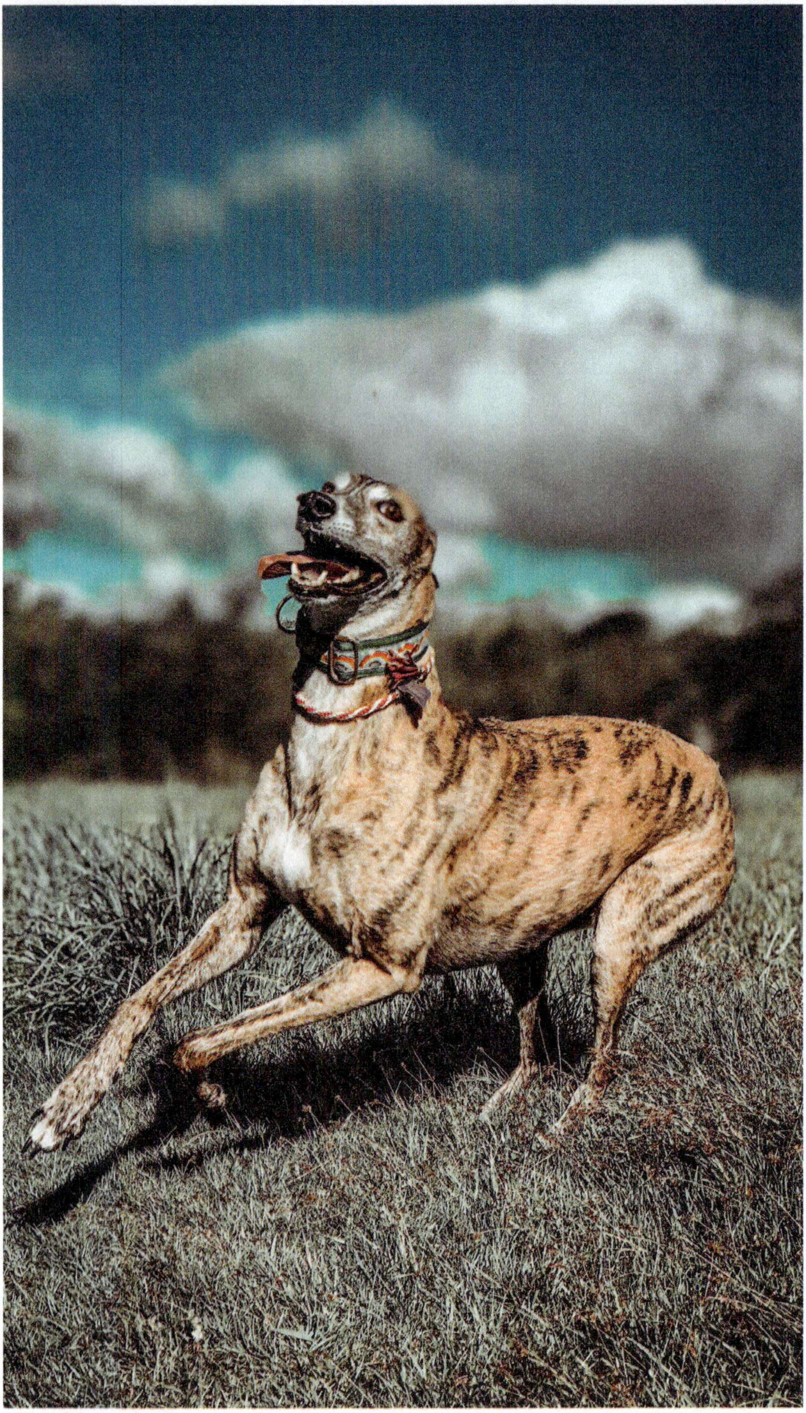

P O P P Y

One of my favourite photo's, as with all photos come context. Here, Poppy has a medical issue undiagnosed at this point. She is restricted to short walks but can't resist having a mad moment, which thankfully I managed to capture.

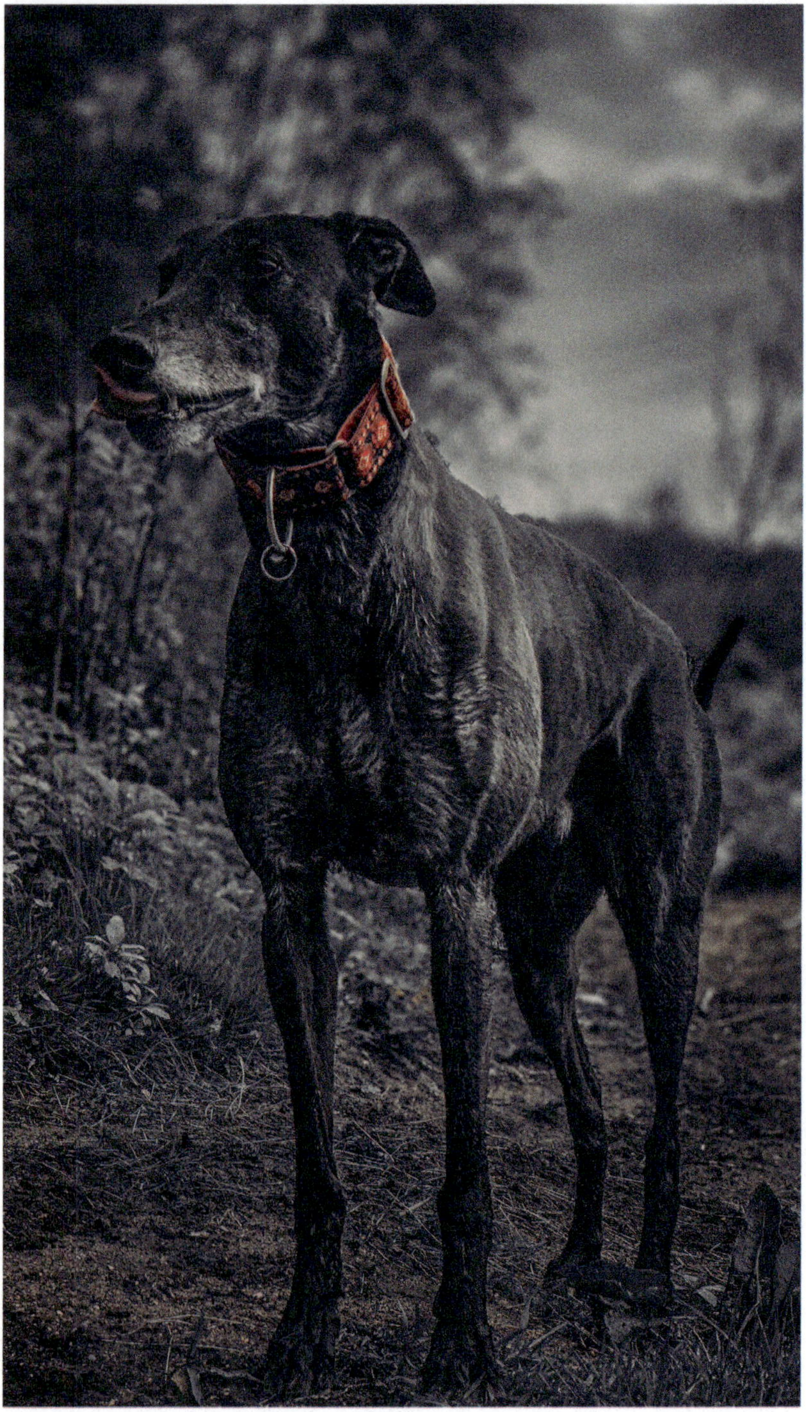

BUDDY

Black dogs proved notably difficult to photograph, and this held true for Buddy as well. His skill at evading the camera made it tough to capture him. Thus, I was especially pleased when he momentarily halted, allowing me to snap this picture.

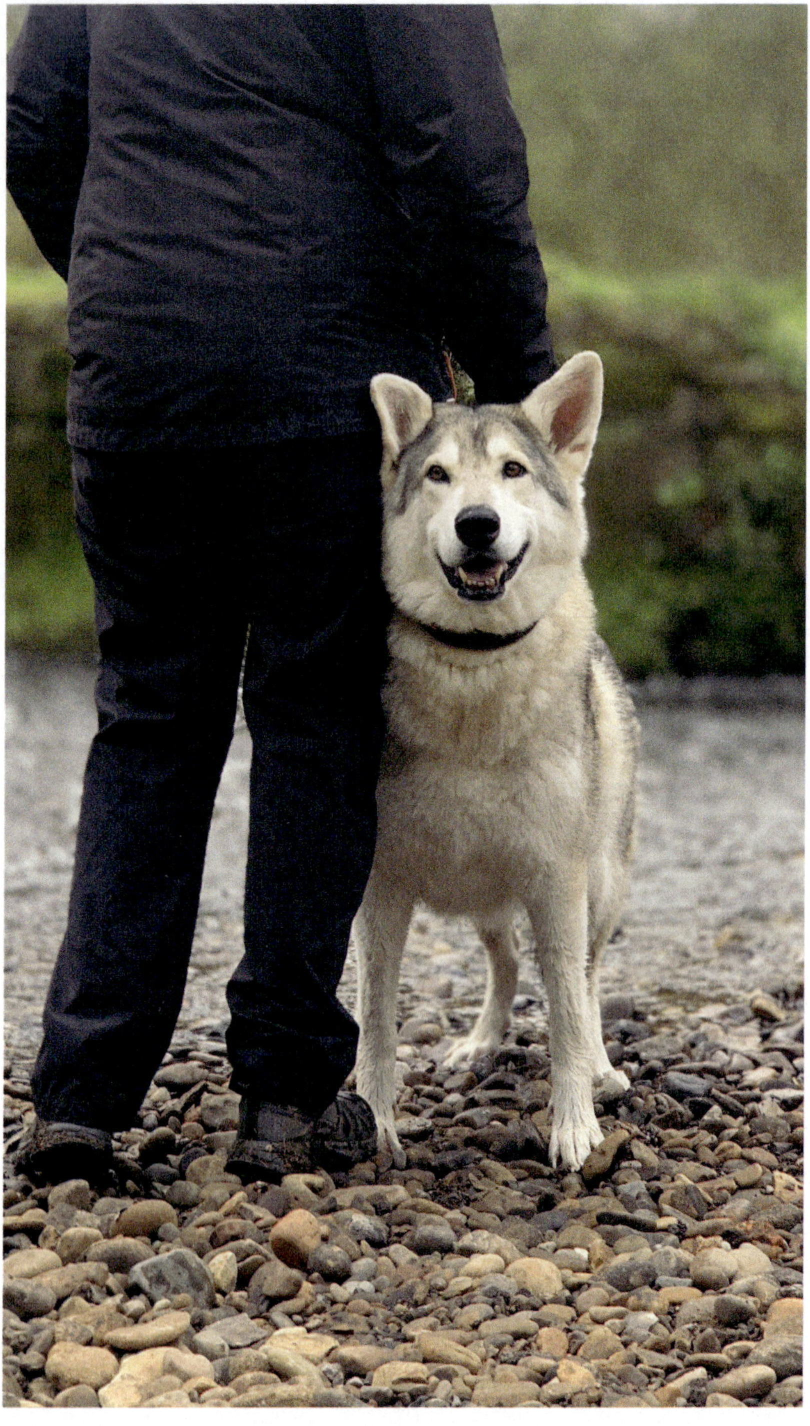

TIKAANI

Tikaani, or "big man" or "T," is the most vocal dog I know, yet a soft-hearted giant. While I possess numerous pictures of him showcasing his commanding aura, I treasure this one—capturing him having a sneaky cuddle with one of his mum's.

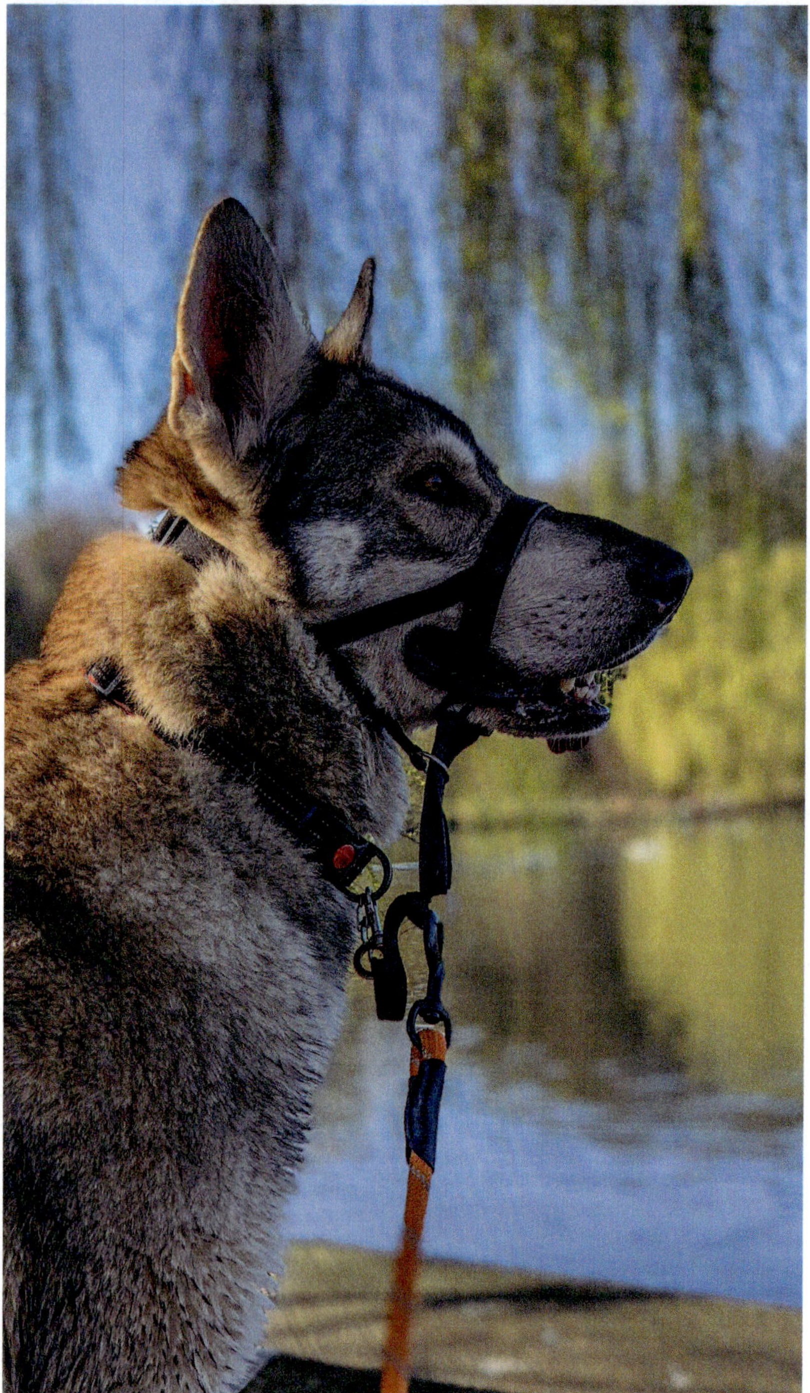

K A I

Kai is a big guy, sometimes a bit eager, but he means well. He's a fan of cuddles and loves a ball. His best mate is Tikaani, but here it was just him and me on a walk. He stopped for a moment, enjoyed the view, and posed for me with a smile.

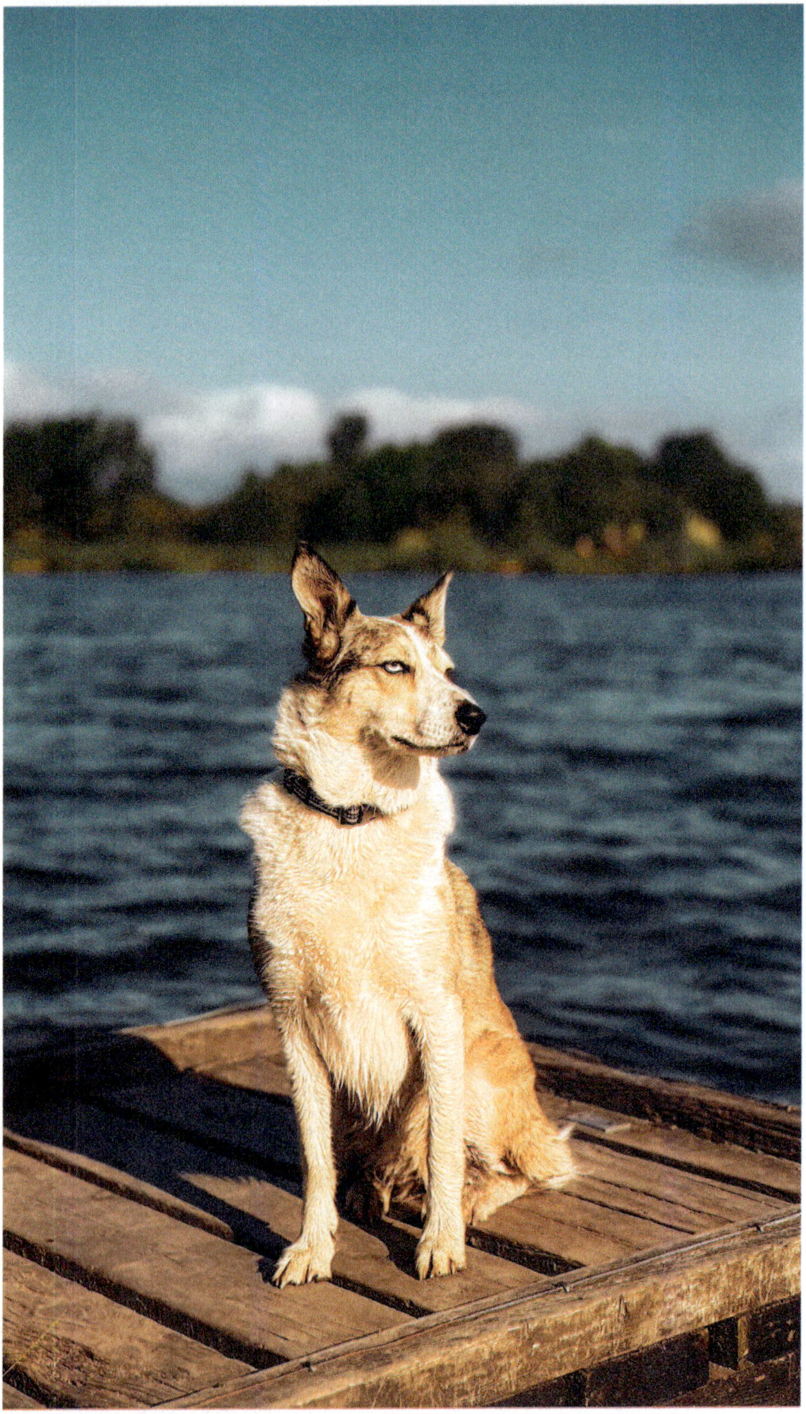

MOLLIE

I've taught Mollie how to pose for photos, making others quite envious at times. She's probably tired of my constant picture-taking. In this shot, she's relaxing in a cool breeze during one of our walks near the fishing lodge.

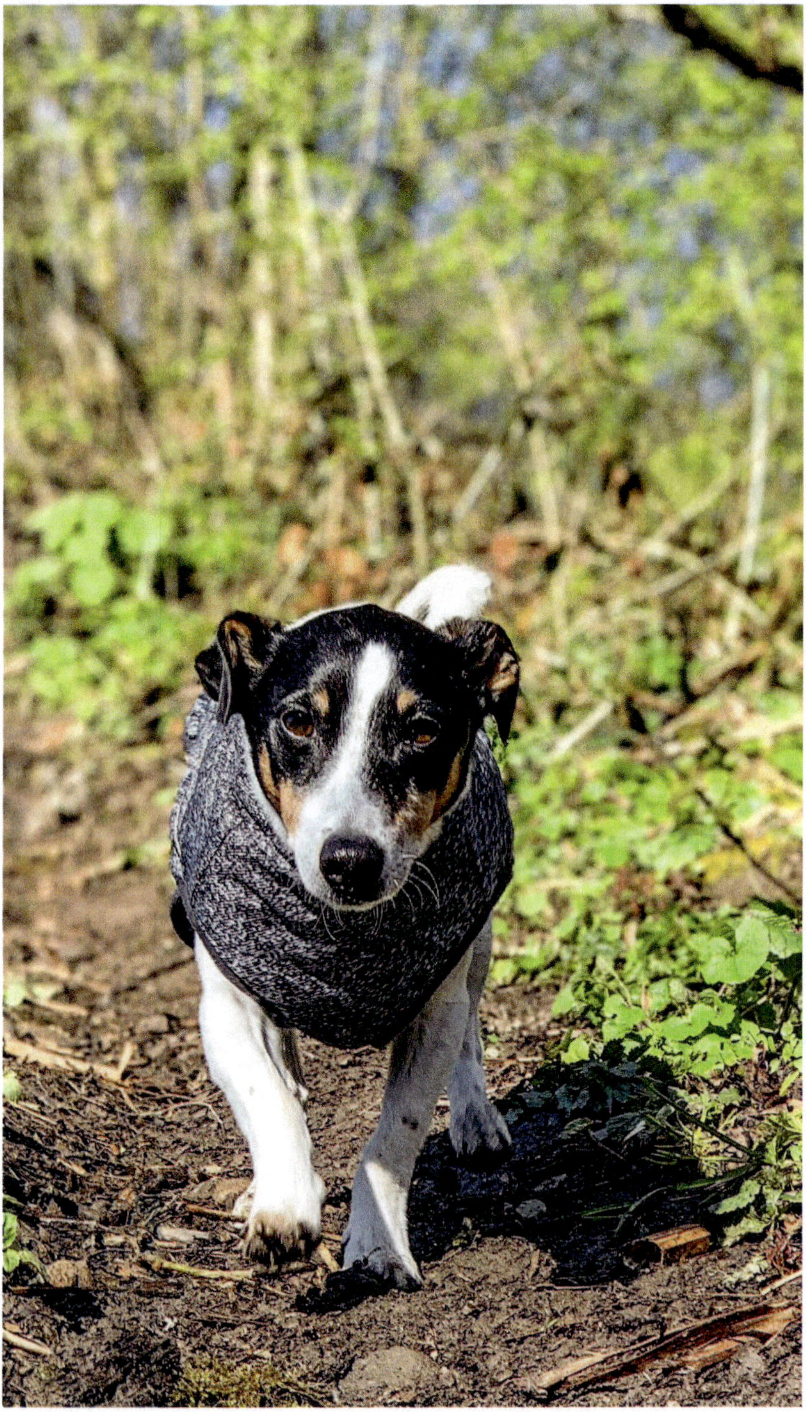

BORIS

I received my fair share of scoldings, rightfully, for not capturing enough photos of Boris. His impeccable behavior and low stature would often make me overlook him. Nevertheless, my affection for him remains unwavering, a pleasure to be around.

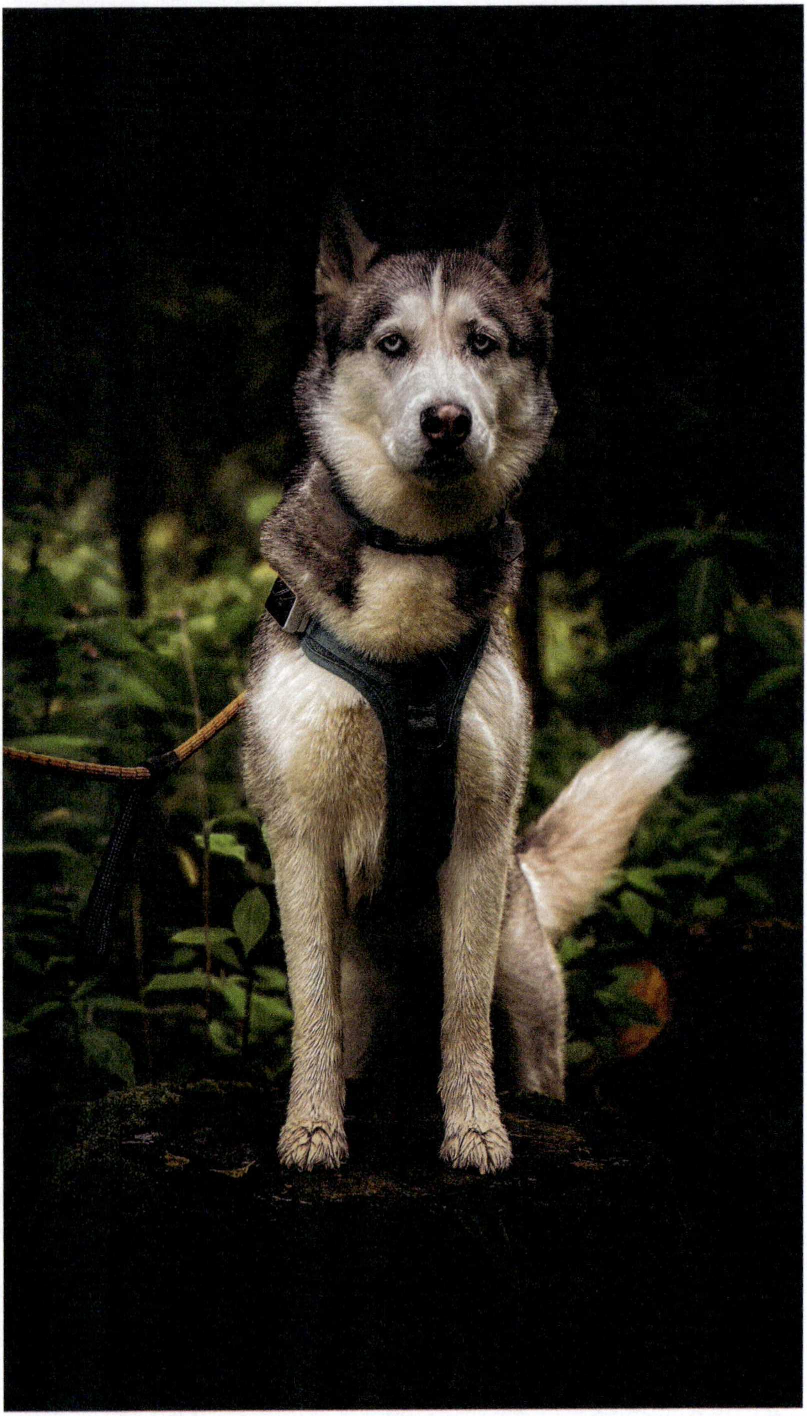

MISTY

I was genuinely happy with this photo. Misty, the second most talkative dog I'm acquainted with, has a way of announcing treat time and demanding attention. However, in this instance, she momentarily posed for me so I could capture this shot.

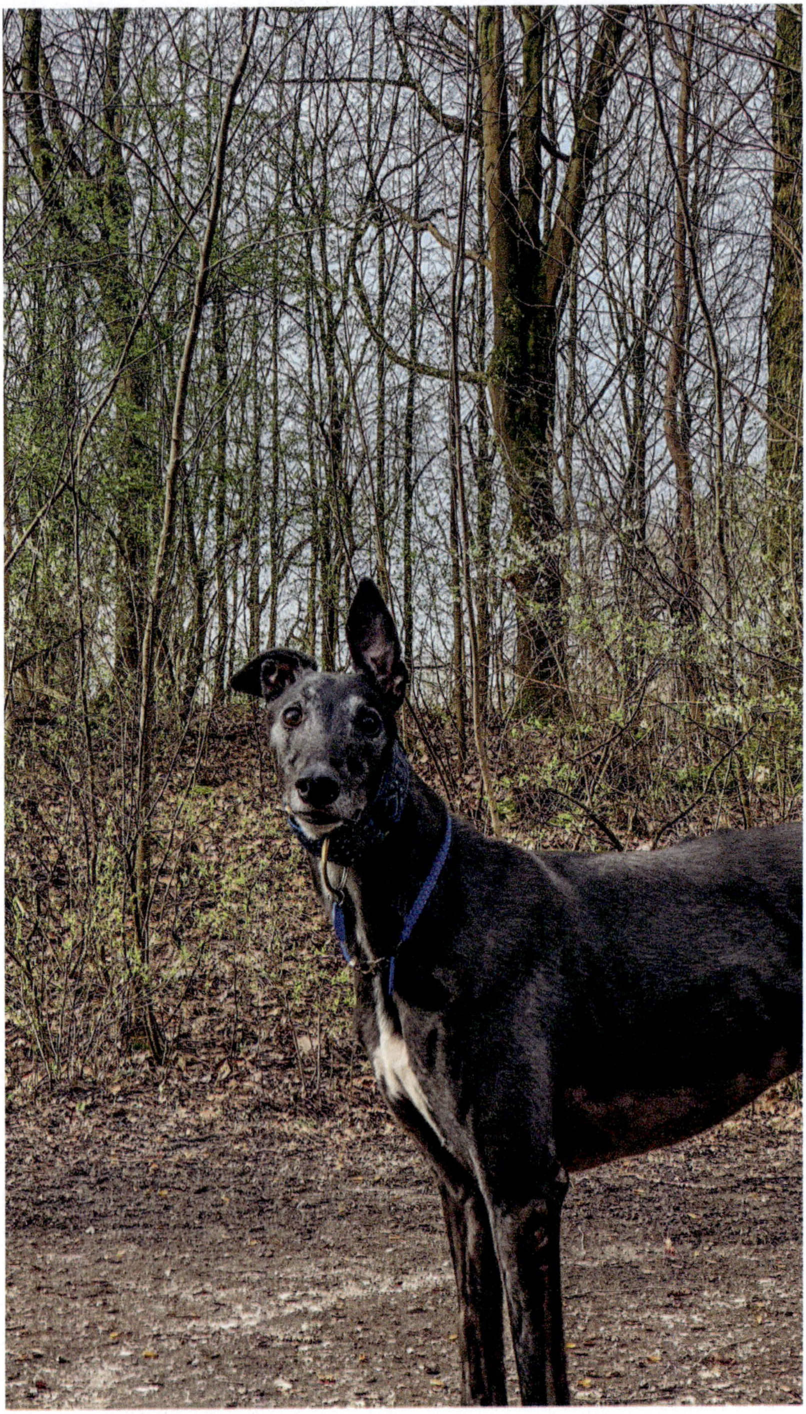

BUDGE

Budge stood as the tallest, yet most elusive dog for my photography endeavours. Every now and then, he'd stop for a treat, giving me a chance for a quick snapshot. He sadly crossed over in early 2023. Rest in peace, big man, you're still missed.

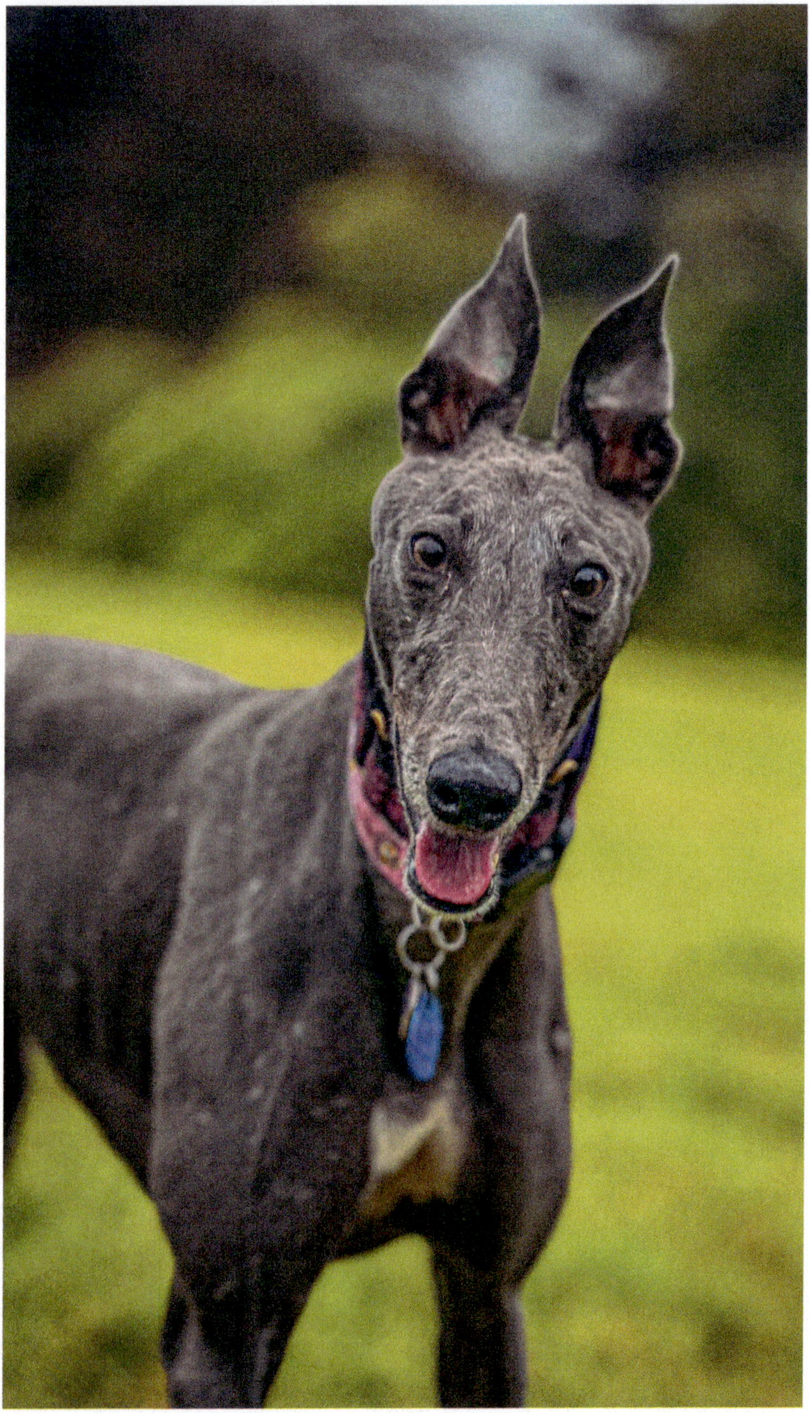

JODIE

Jodie started as a foster dog for Sharon, eventually being adopted and became my second most photographed dog after Mollie. She is Facebook famous due to her lively antics and expressive face, she is now known as "Jodie Foster."

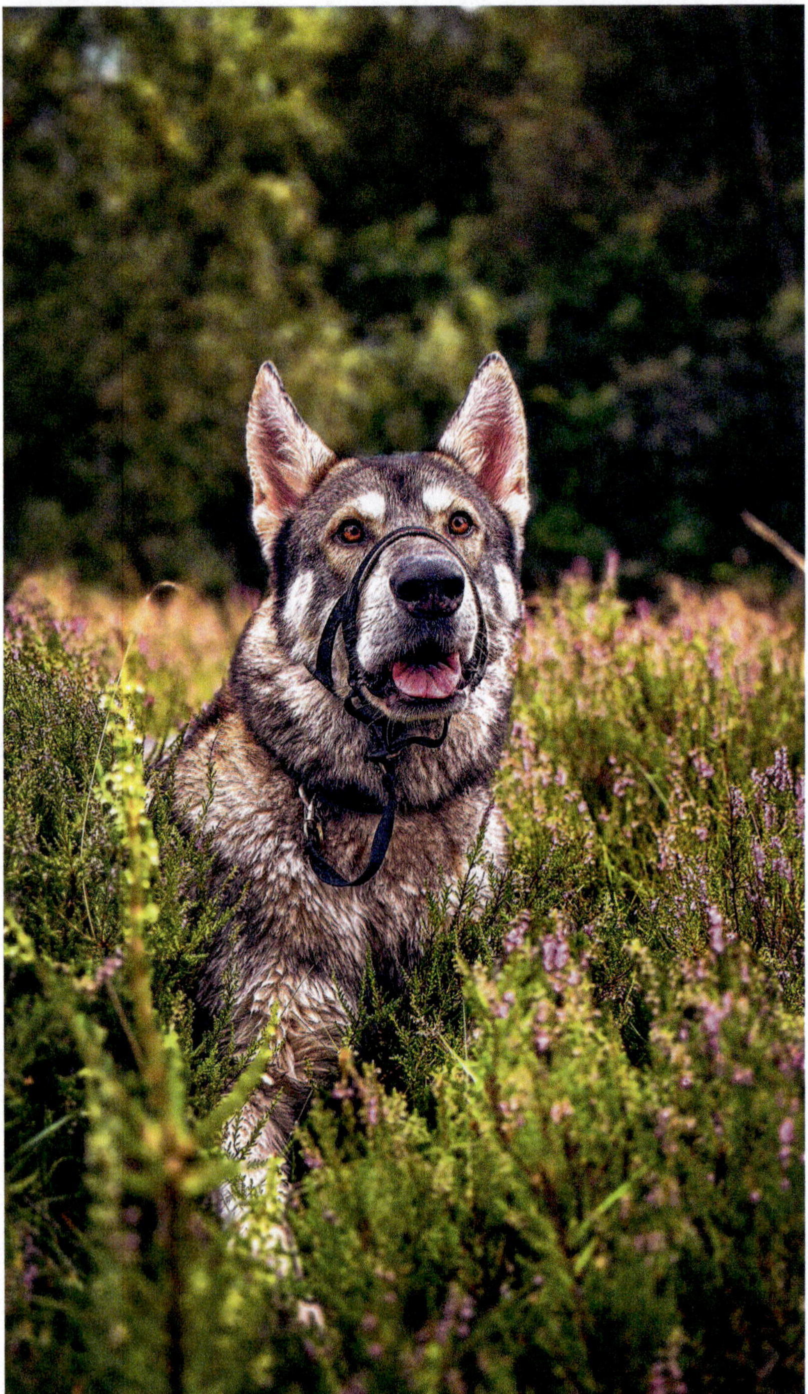

K A I

Here's another shot of Kai, a rare instance of him actually lying down for a photo. I captured this very recently and couldn't resist including it in the book. The photo won't convey the full aroma, though – he had rolled in something quite pungent.

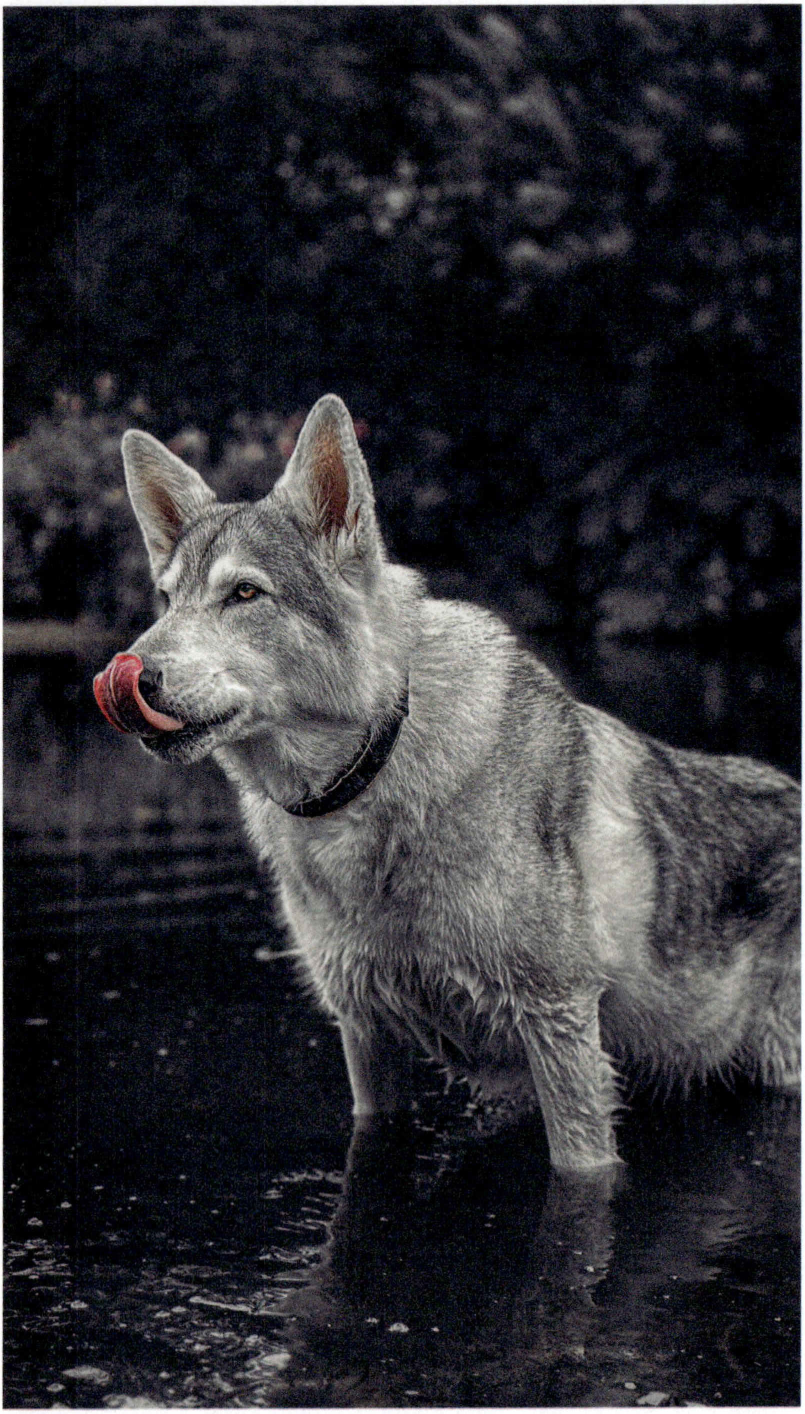

TIKAANI

Here's another recent picture that I couldn't pass up including. Tikaani is a natural in front of the camera; he even had a movie offer at one point, if I remember correctly. Here his eyes are well and truly focused on an incoming treat.

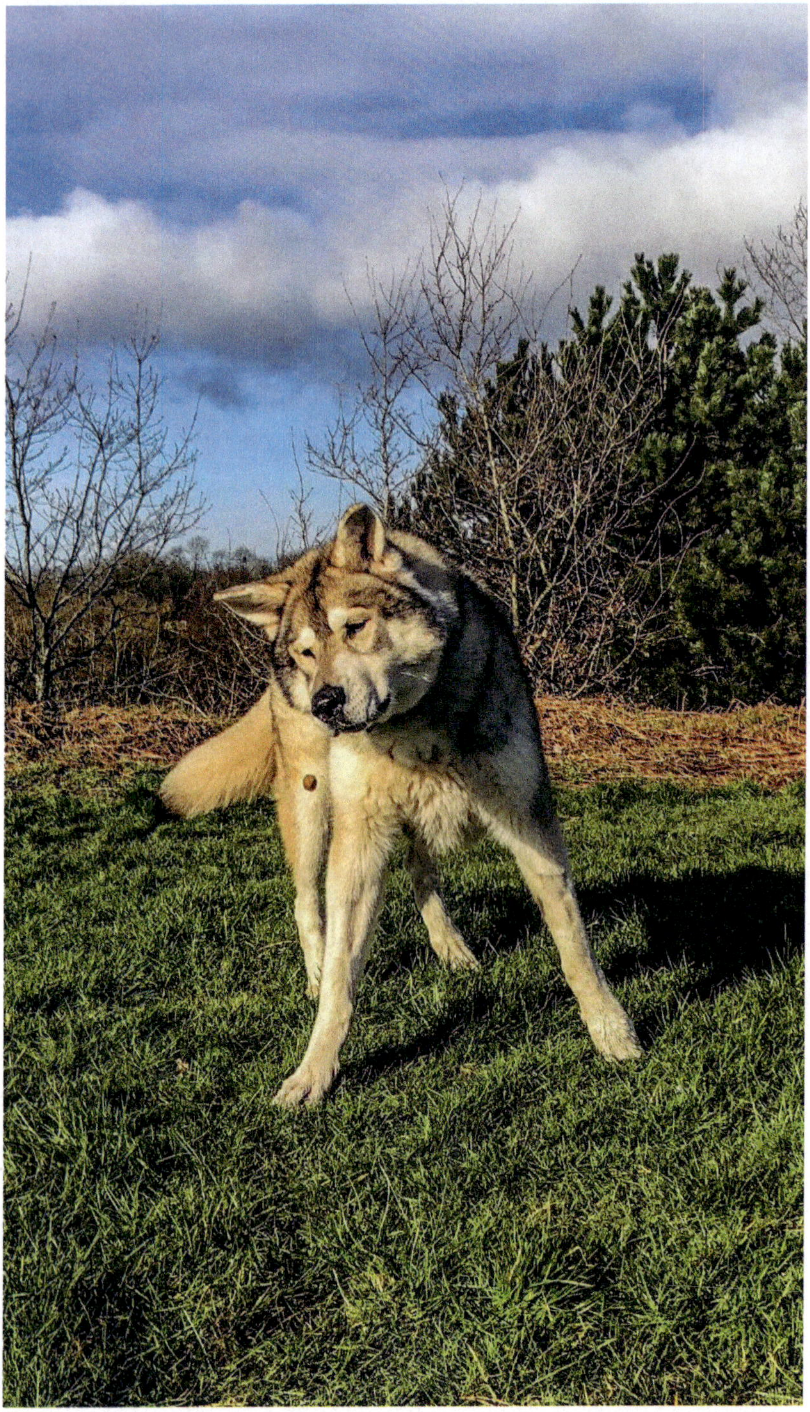

K O D I

Although I didn't know him for long, I had a strong affection for Kodi who to me resembled a bear. He loved a cuddle and strangely tolerated Mollie playfully nipping at his ears. Rest in peace, Kodi, you remain unforgotten and loved.

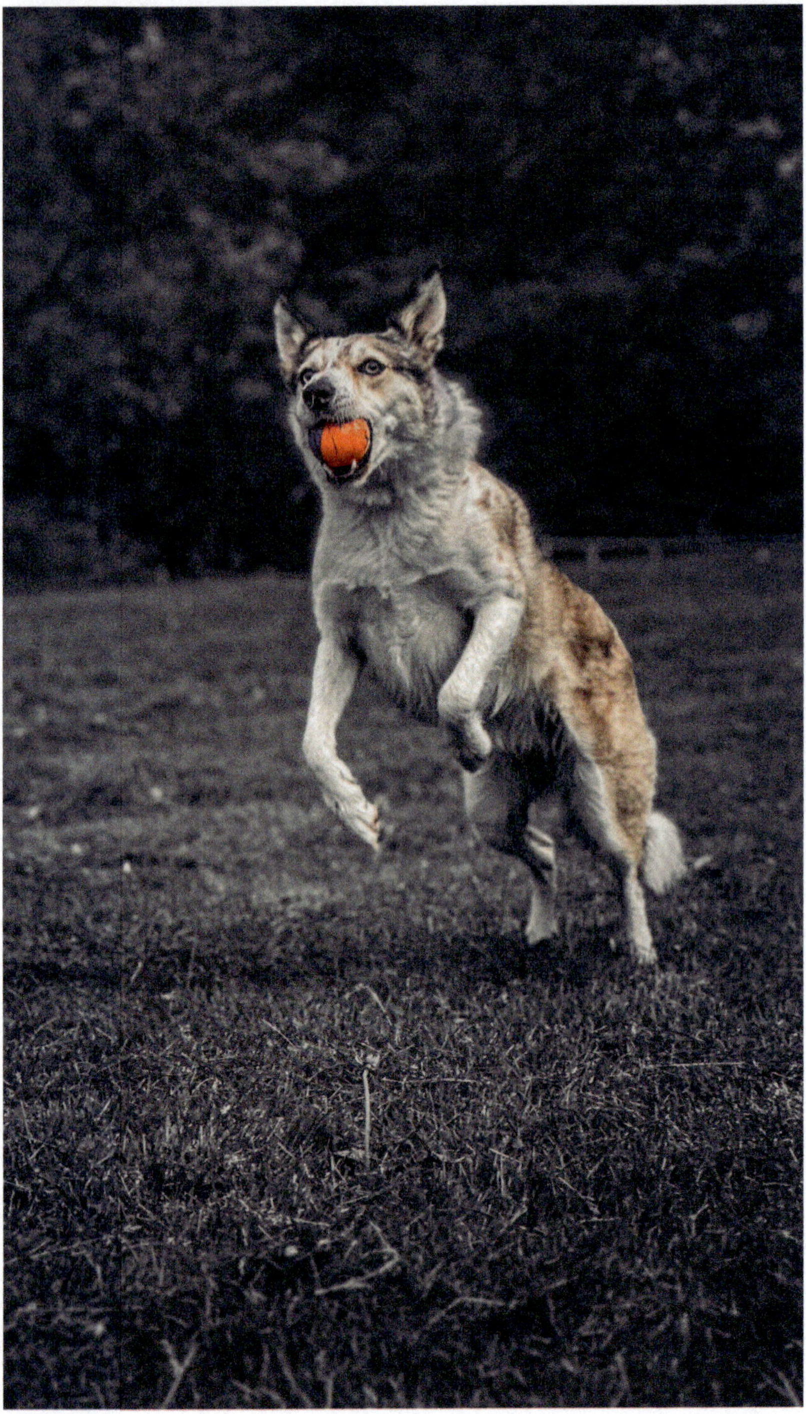

MOLLIE

Since it's my book, I'm indulging in as many Mollie pictures as I please, haha. One of my cherished pastimes with Mollie was snapping her in mid-air as she caught the ball, just like you can see here. *Ball provided by Sarah after Kai ate Mollies.

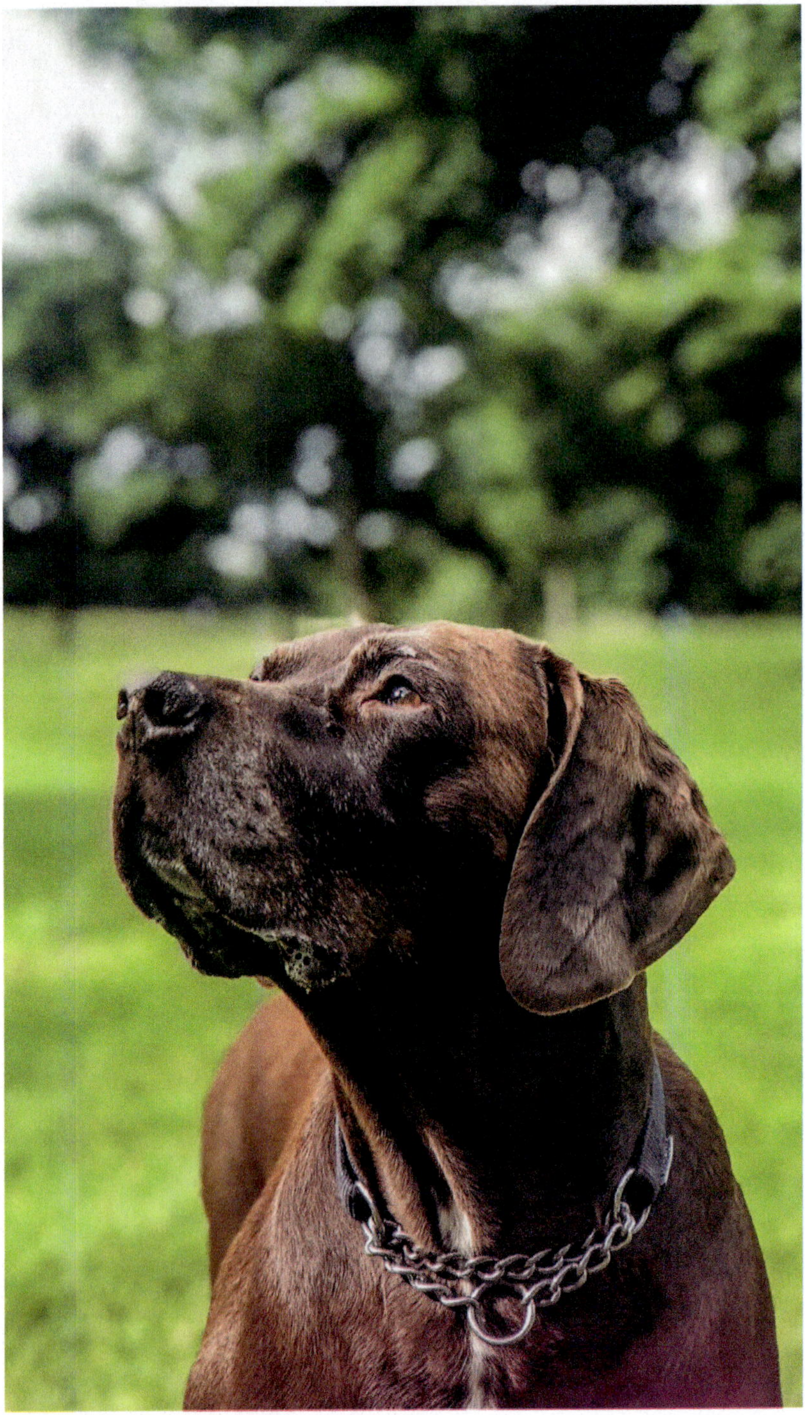

R U B Y

Ruby was a seasoned member of the Demics even before I joined, but she had some years ahead. Despite her age, she remained active and relished a good swim—her element, it seemed. Unfortunately, we recently bid farewell to her. Rest in peace, Ruby.

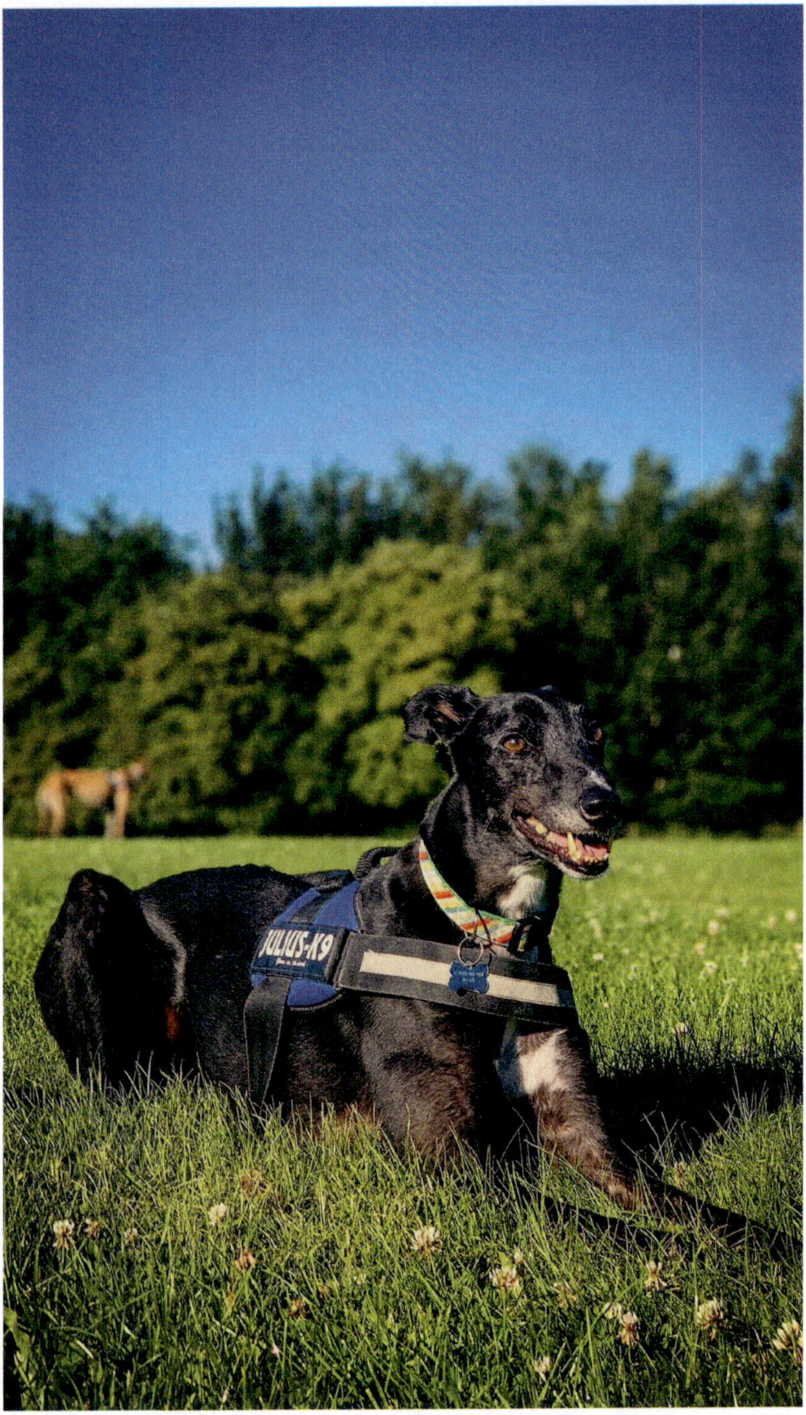
JULIUS-K9

TEDDY

Teddy proves to be quite the challenge to capture on camera. Slow-moving but camera-shy, with his black fur making lighting a challenge. Fortunately, on this beautiful day, he decided to lie down and give me a smile.

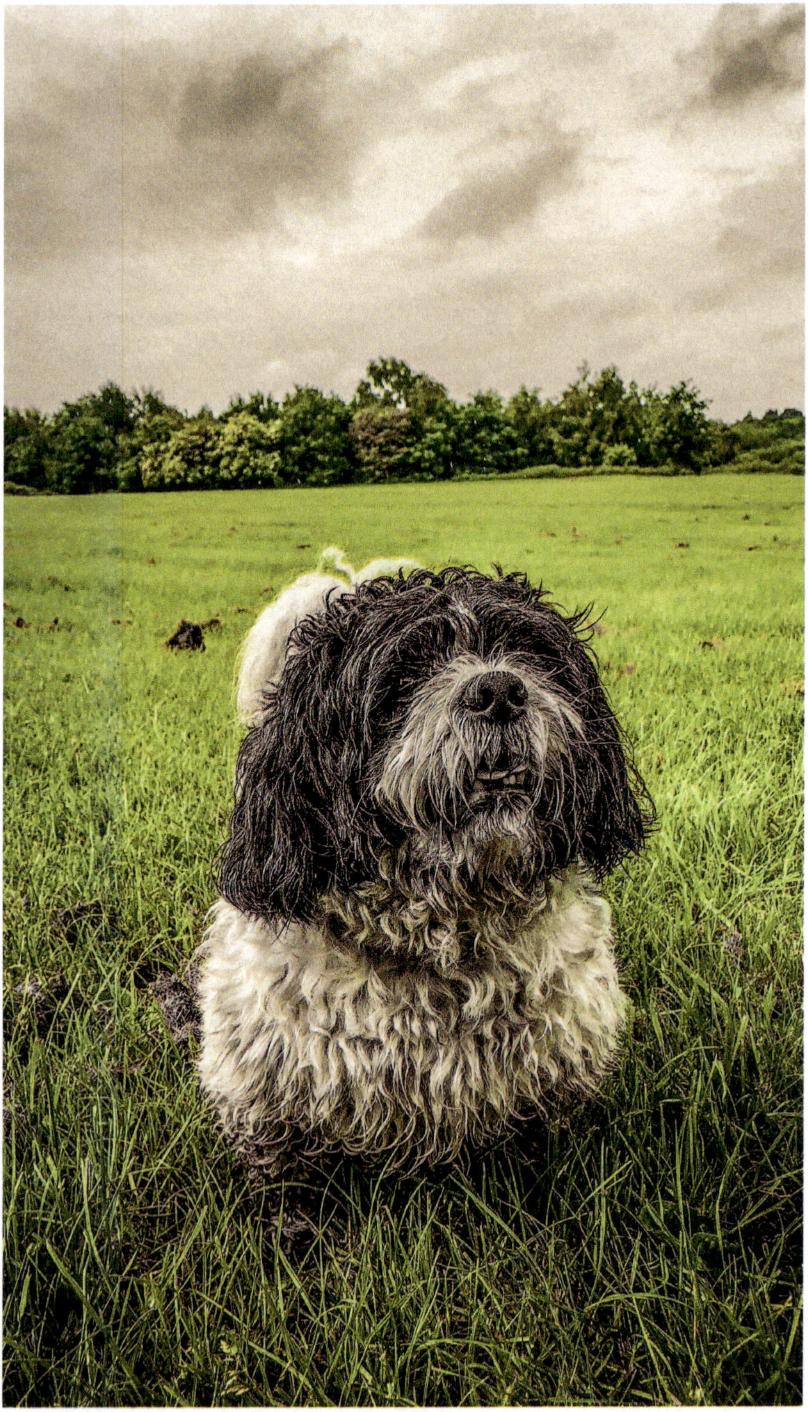

P   I

Pi was under Jude's care, a leisurely mover who frequently lagged behind, prompting us to backtrack and wait. Nonetheless, he held a special place within the group. Regrettably, he is another demic dog we recently bid farewell to.

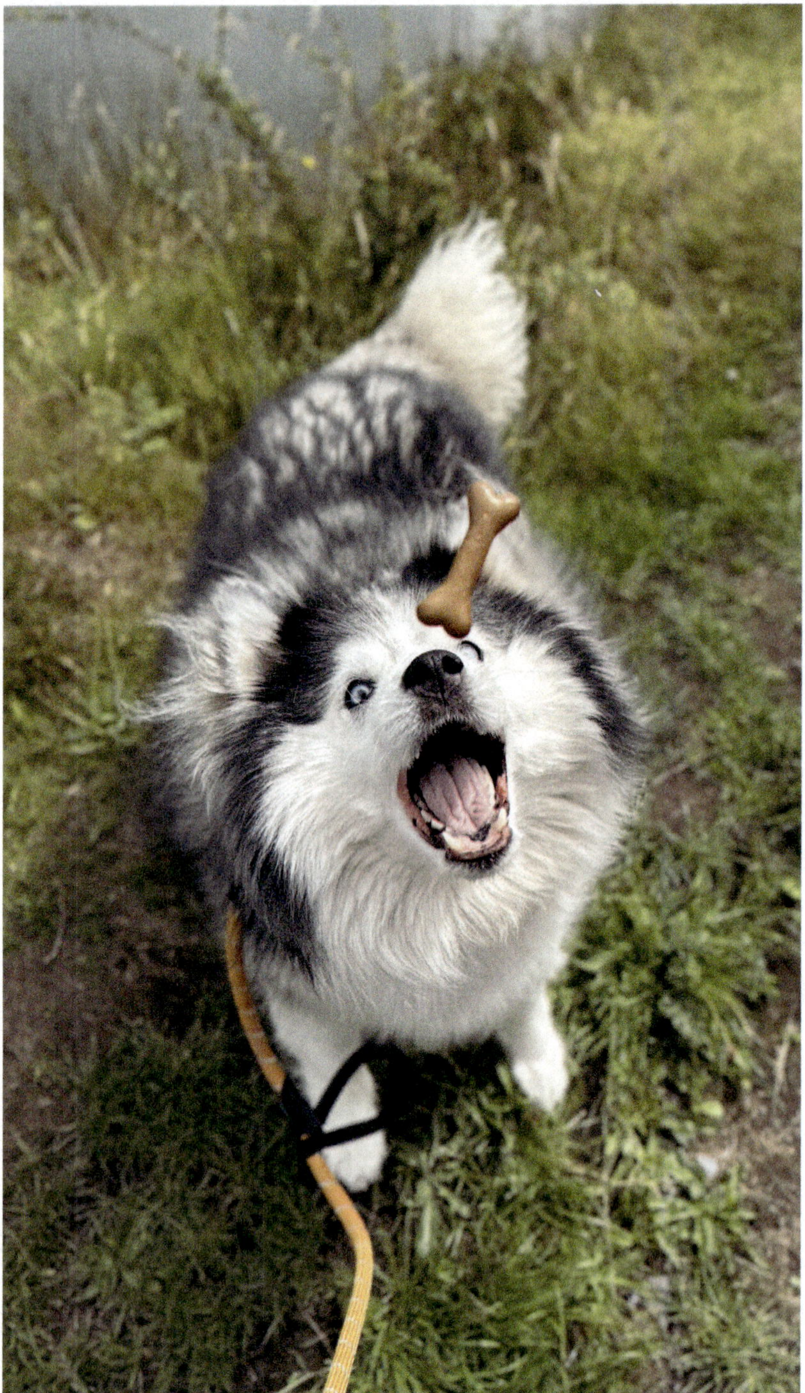

S K Y

Sky swiftly became my favourite customer dog, earning her rightful spot in this book. As an older Husky, she favoured leisurely strolls. Exceptionally gentle, photogenic, and with a touch of diva charm, she 'had me at hello'.

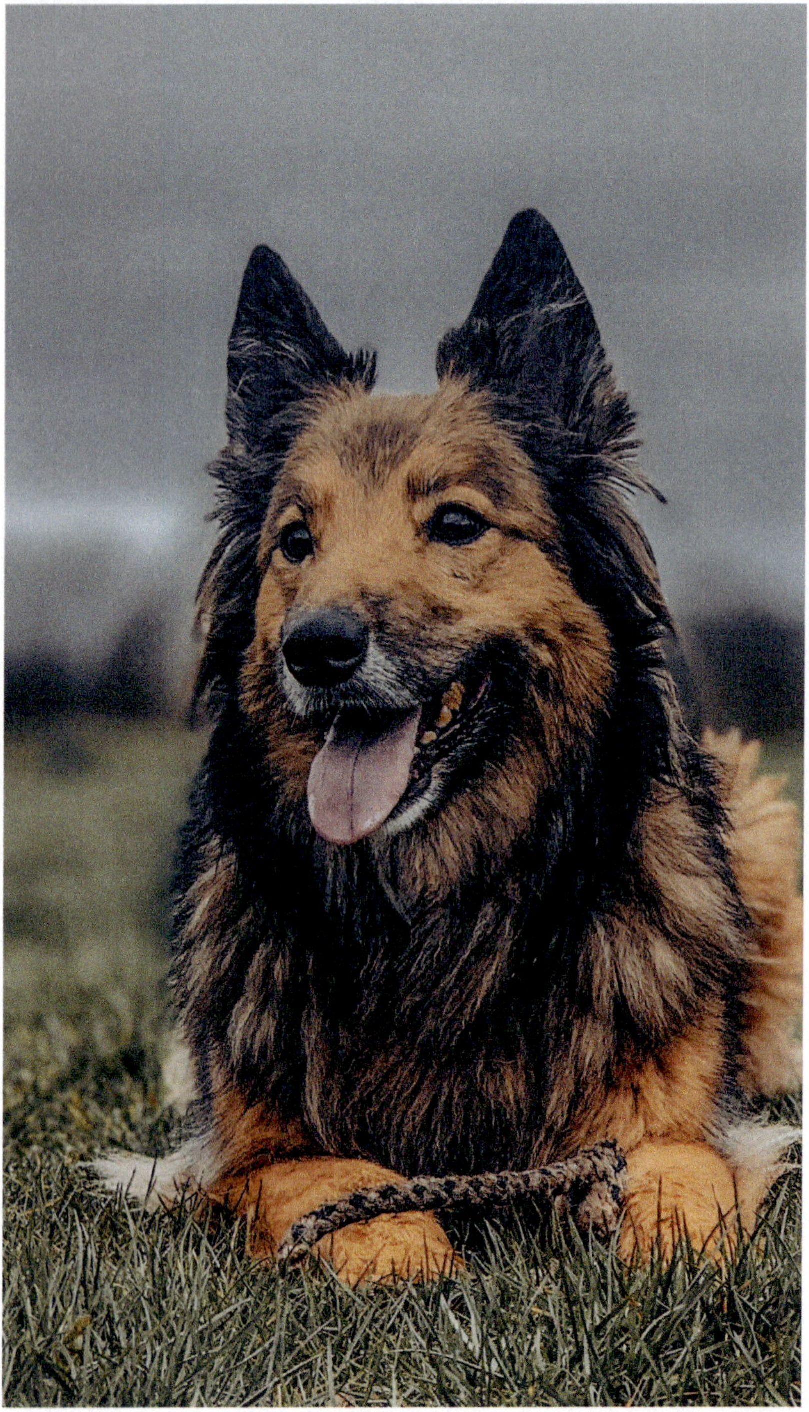

M A R A

Mara stands out for her remarkable intelligence and boundless vitality. Her agility is so remarkable that capturing a photo of her is a rare feat, but in this instance, she took a moment to lie down, allowing me to capture a fleeting snapshot.

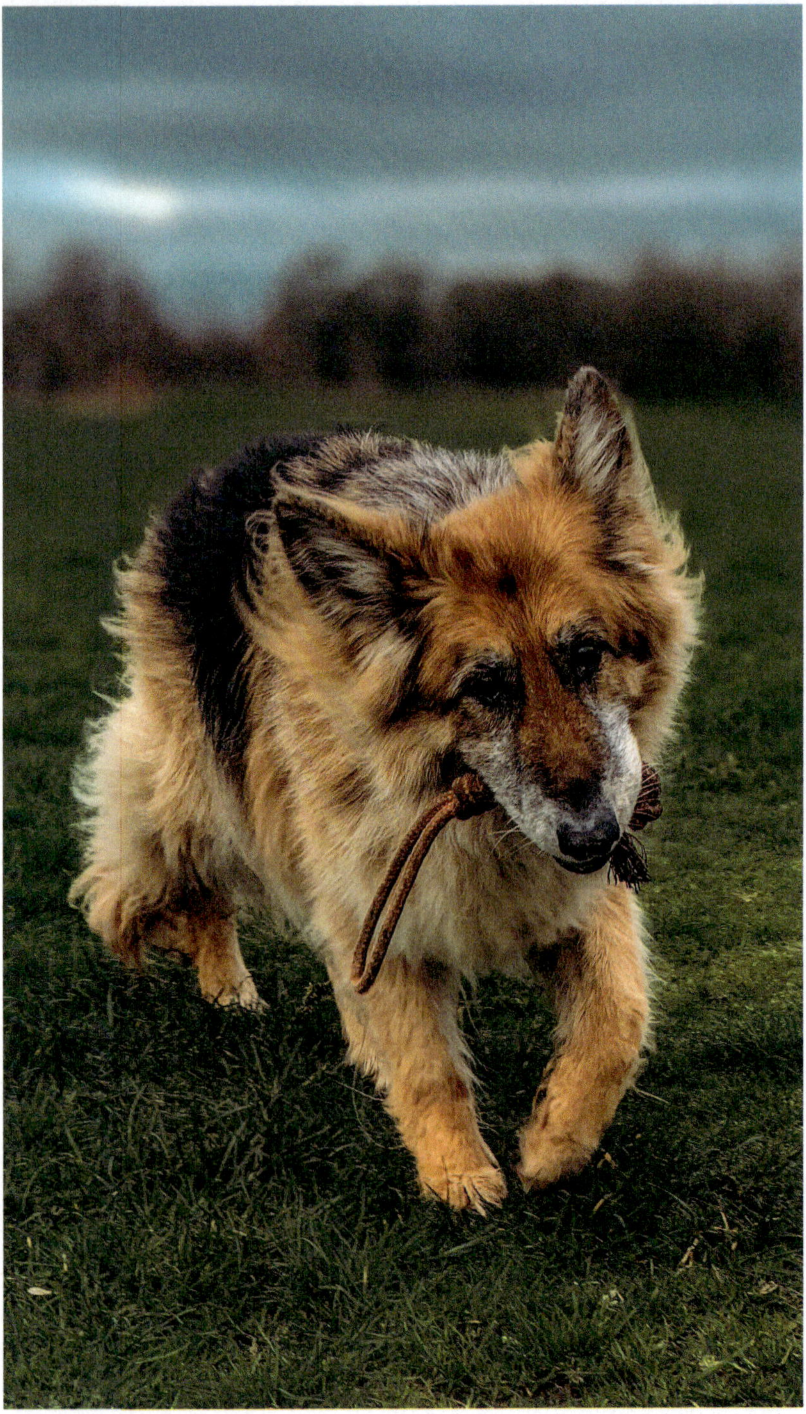

LEX

Lex was another canine with remarkable intelligence. His time with us sadly came to an end as I wrote this book. Clever, affectionate, with his own set of quirks, just about everything you could ever wish for in a dog.

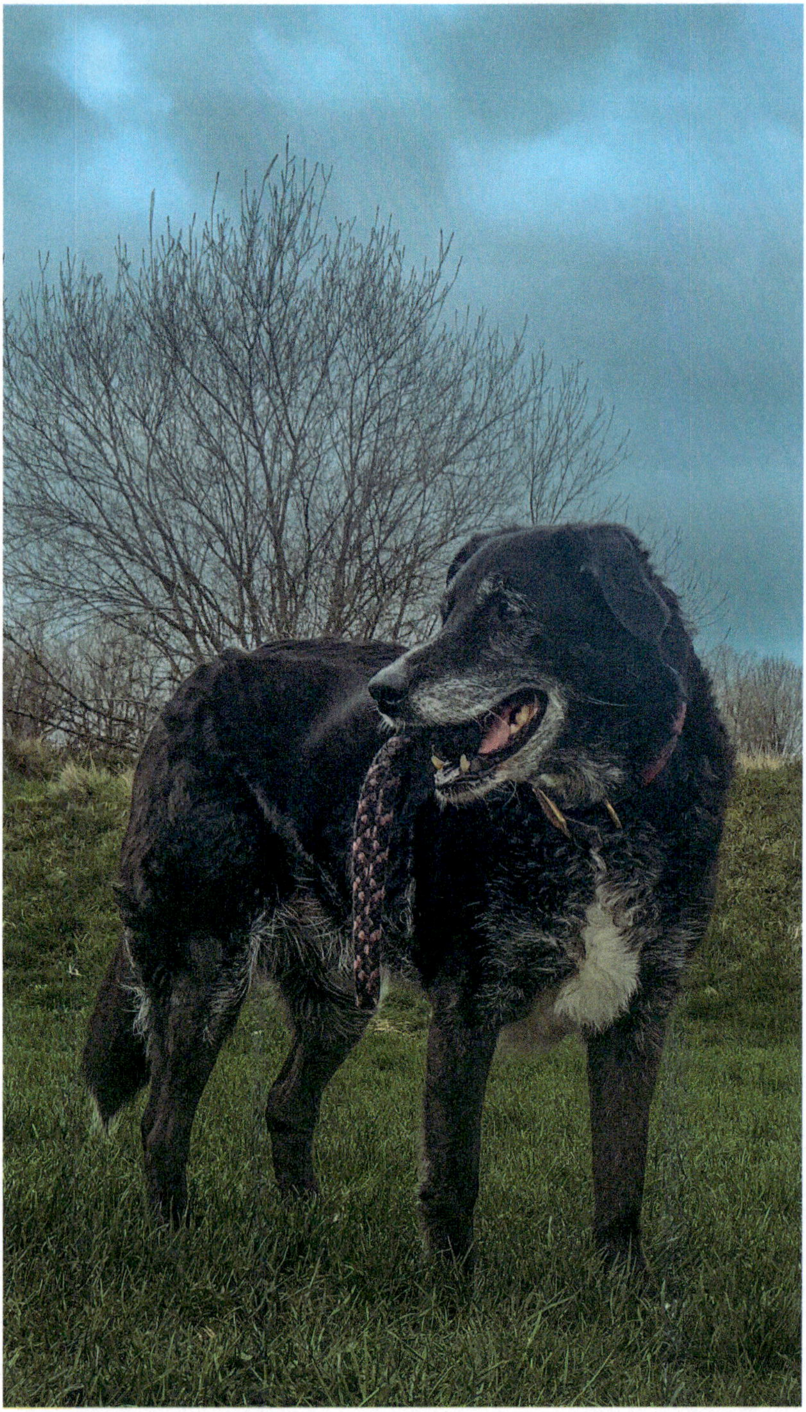

ANNIE

Annie proves to be one of the most challenging dogs I've tried to photograph. Her black fur adds to the difficulty, and she often appears to be turned away from the camera. She spends her days with Lex and Mara and loses her ball regularly.

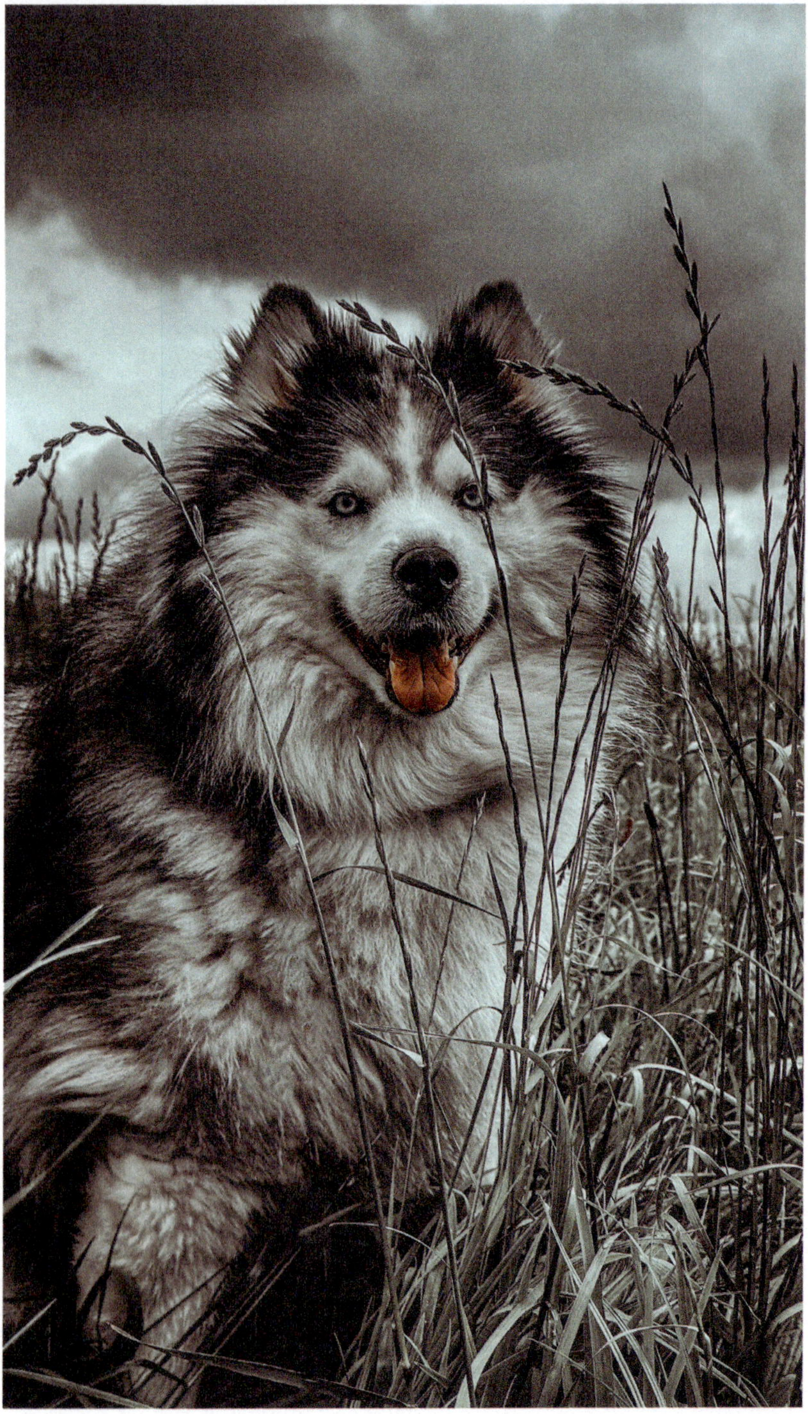

S K Y

As my most favourite dog among all my customers, Sky rightfully claims a couple of spots in this book. Seeing her always brings a smile to my face, cuddles are her favourite, and she's almost always ready to strike a pose for the camera.

Feeling better

As the days went by, I could sense a genuine improvement in my overall well-being. Of course, there were still those moments when I felt a bit low, but I was learning to handle them with a newfound resilience. I granted myself permission to experience those occasional down days, even indulging in a chocolate binge if the mood struck. The difference was, I no longer allowed a single day of feeling down to snowball into an extended period of darkness. If I ever felt myself teetering on the edge of a week-long slump, I took proactive steps to assess the situation. I'd check in with myself: had I shared my feelings with anyone recently? If not, I'd make a call to my mum, have a heart-to-heart with my grandma, or reach out to a friend if I felt up to it. Sometimes, all it took was a meaningful conversation to lift my spirits and remind me that I wasn't navigating this journey alone. Other times, it was about recalibrating my interests and activities. Did I need to embark on a bike ride, engage in a drawing session, or perhaps dive into a writing project? The world was filled with possibilities, and I was beginning to embrace them all as tools for managing my emotional well-being.

Dog walking had become a source of unadulterated joy for me, and it was evident to anyone who saw Mollie and me bounding around during our walks. Despite Mollie's eccentricities at home, our outdoor adventures were filled with excitement and happiness. Yet, there was a looming anxiety that began to surface when I contemplated leaving her for any extended period – even for a few hours or the duration of a wedding. Would anyone else be able to handle her quirky split personality? Was I just overthinking things? As I navigated this internal struggle by opting to limit my time away from her, it sparked an idea that gradually took root. Why not channel this passion and appreciation for the outdoors, dog walking, and photography into something more than a personal pursuit? The question began to germinate in my mind – could I turn this trifecta of joy into a business? The more I pondered the idea, the more it seemed like a natural evolution. After all, I was already living proof that these elements could bring happiness, and perhaps others could benefit from the same formula.

And so, with the seeds of inspiration planted, I set out on a new journey – one that would combine my love for dogs, the great outdoors, and photography into a unique and fulfilling venture. Little did I know that this venture would not only reshape my career path but also serve as a conduit for personal growth and continued healing. In crafting my dog walking business, I was determined to carve out a path that aligned with my values and eased my anxiety rather than exacerbating it. Online, I encountered the prevailing trend of dog walkers corralling multiple dogs at once, sometimes in dauntingly large packs of six, seven, or even more. It left me pondering the logistics and ethics of such an approach – how could one possibly ensure the well-being and behaviour of so many dogs in unison? My concerns deepened as I witnessed a woman struggling to manage ten dogs at once. The thought crossed my mind: What if one ran off? How could she guarantee their safety and happiness?

Curiosity drove me to delve into the legality of this practice. The law, varying slightly by local councils, generally stipulated a limit of four dogs per walker. It became evident that many were surpassing this threshold. My intention, however, was never to break the law or compromise the well-being of the dogs. I suffered from anxiety, and my aim was to create a venture that alleviated stress rather than compounded it. Thus, I resolved to adopt a different business model – one that allowed me to focus entirely on the dogs in my care. I decided to walk just one or two dogs from the same household at a time. This way, I could give them my undivided attention, ensuring their comfort, safety, and individual needs were met. Moreover, this approach resonated with dog owners who faced similar concerns – their pets might be anxious, aggressive around other dogs, or simply not up to the pace of a group walk. My dedication to one-on-one interaction and my passion for photography became my unique selling proposition (USP). I took this philosophy to heart, understanding that quality care could never be compromised by quantity.

This wasn't meant to be a full-time endeavour – rather, it was designed to break the monotony of desk work and provide a fulfilling way to spend my days. My routine came alive: walking Mollie, engaging in work, venturing out for one-on-one dog walks, all the while fitting in bike rides as I commuted between customers' houses. This regimen not only alleviated my anxiety but also improved my overall fitness. By focusing on the dogs' well-being, my mental and physical health experienced a transformation.

With my dog walking business well underway, I was committed to not just fulfilling my responsibilities but also deriving genuine joy from each walk. While capturing photographs of the dogs allowed me to document these moments, I felt a growing urge to expand my creative endeavours. My thirst for exploration led me to delve into various forms of photography and videography, embracing new niches like nature, wildlife, and urban photography.

In order to truly appreciate and savour each walk, I initiated a practice I coined as "mindful moments." Every time I ventured out, I challenged myself to discover a picturesque scene that resonated with me – a tranquil riverbank, the playfulness of sunlight filtering through leaves, or the striking contrast of an urban landscape. With my camera in hand, I'd capture these fleeting scenes, dedicating anywhere from 20 seconds to a minute to encapsulate the essence of the moment.

This practice served as a powerful tool to ground me in the present. I recognised the profound blessing of being outdoors, even when the rain came pouring down. In those moments, I'd remind myself that this was the essence of tranquillity – an opportunity to immerse myself in the natural world and find solace in its embrace. This journey of mindfulness led me off the well-trodden paths and into more uncharted territories.

My exploration led me to cross paths with some precious inhabitants of the natural world – goslings and cygnets. I stumbled upon baby geese and swans during my walks and decided to take it upon myself to provide them with sustenance. Each day, I'd bring food to feed these young creatures, fostering a bond that transcended human-animal interactions. After a few weeks, they began to recognise the sound of my bike bell, emerging from the canal waters in anticipation of their mealtime. It was a testament to the connections that could be forged when we engaged with the world around us on a mindful and compassionate level.

While incorporating a mere one-minute mindfulness practice into my daily routine didn't magically eradicate all my bad days, it undeniably provided a crucial anchor. It was about shifting my perspective from simply going through the motions to genuinely cherishing every moment. This wasn't a foolproof solution, but it was certainly a step in the right direction.

The essence of the journey lay in discovering ways to infuse joy into my everyday experiences. It wasn't about merely enduring the day; it was about relishing each moment, whether big or small. And that's the crux of it all – trying out new things, experimenting with different approaches, and determining what resonated with me. It was a process that necessitated a fair share of trial and error.

As I ventured into various activities, I came to realise that finding what truly worked for me wasn't an instant revelation. It might take trying twenty or thirty different things before stumbling upon something that truly struck a chord. But that was the beauty of the process – every new endeavour, whether successful or not, was added to my repertoire of coping mechanisms.

Just as each individual is unique, so too is the path toward healing and self-discovery. The key was to persist, to explore, and to remain open to new experiences. Each addition to my arsenal of defence tools fortified my resilience and bolstered my ability to navigate life's challenges. The journey wasn't linear or without its setbacks, but it was marked by progress and a growing sense of empowerment.

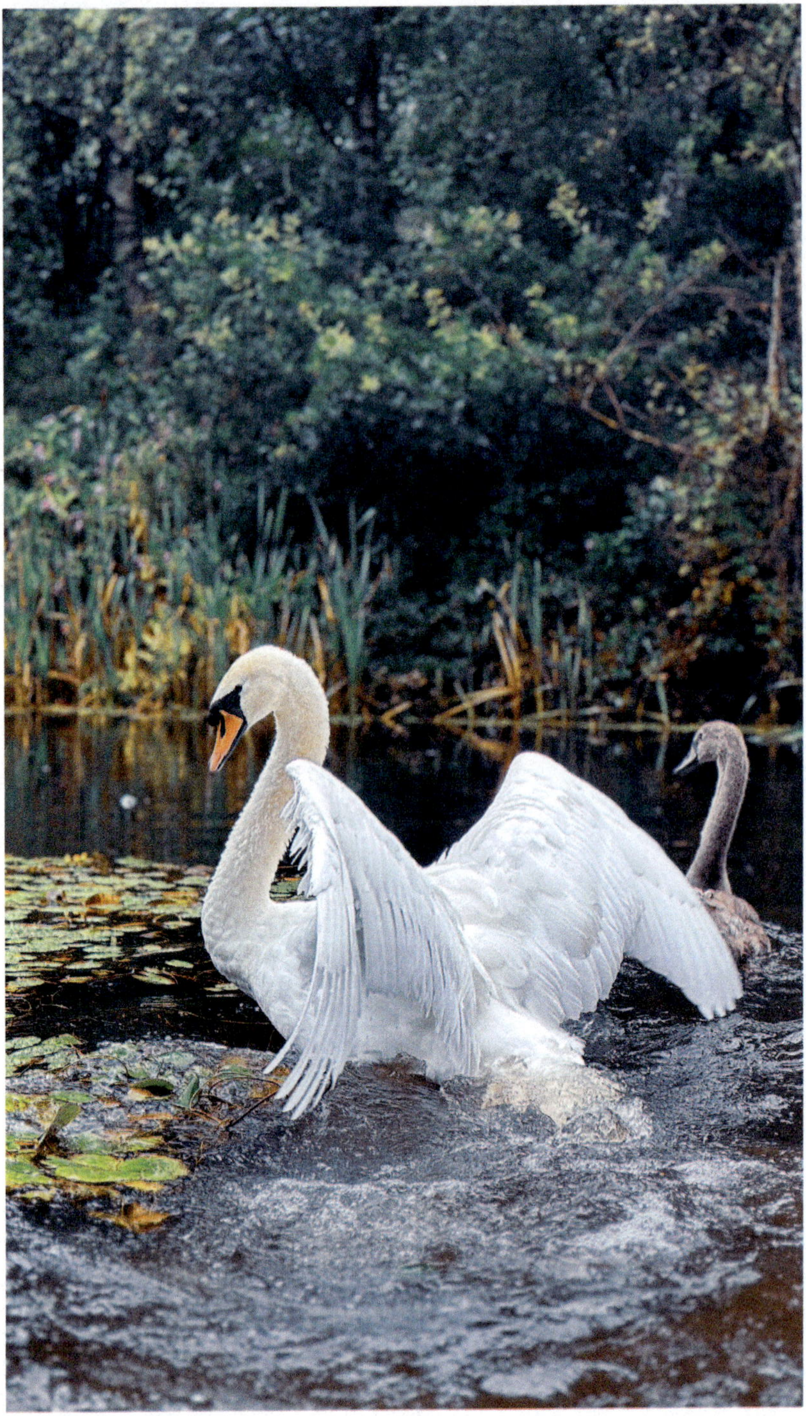

GRACE

"Grace" depicts a serene scene on a pond, where a swan exquisitely fans its wings, creating a picturesque moment of beauty and tranquility. Beside the swan, its precious offspring follows, mirroring the parent's elegant gestures.

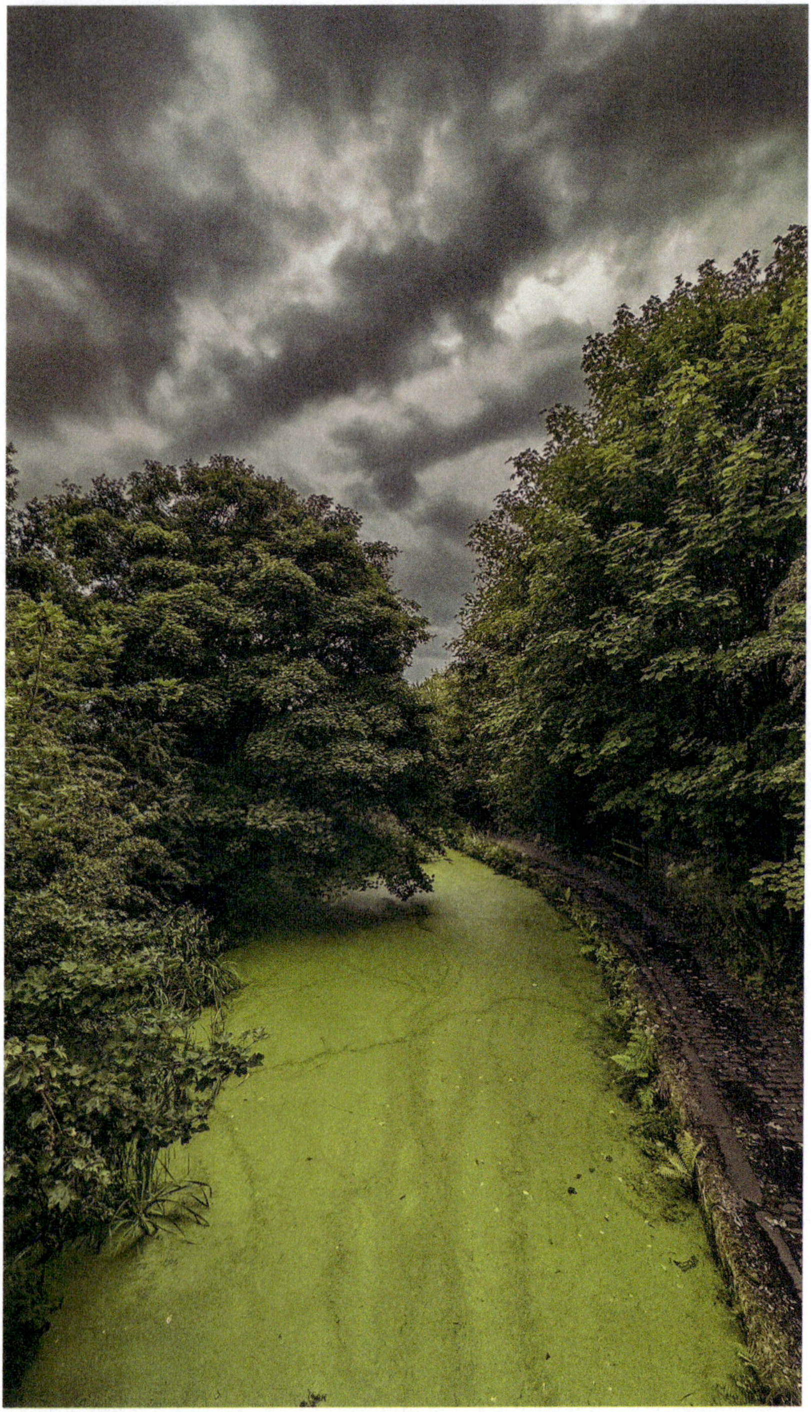

L U S H

Captured from a slightly elevated perspective, the photograph "Lush" unveils a canal with a substantial cover of vibrant green duckweed forming a dense blanket atop the water. Hovering above is an eerie skyline casting a mysterious atmosphere.

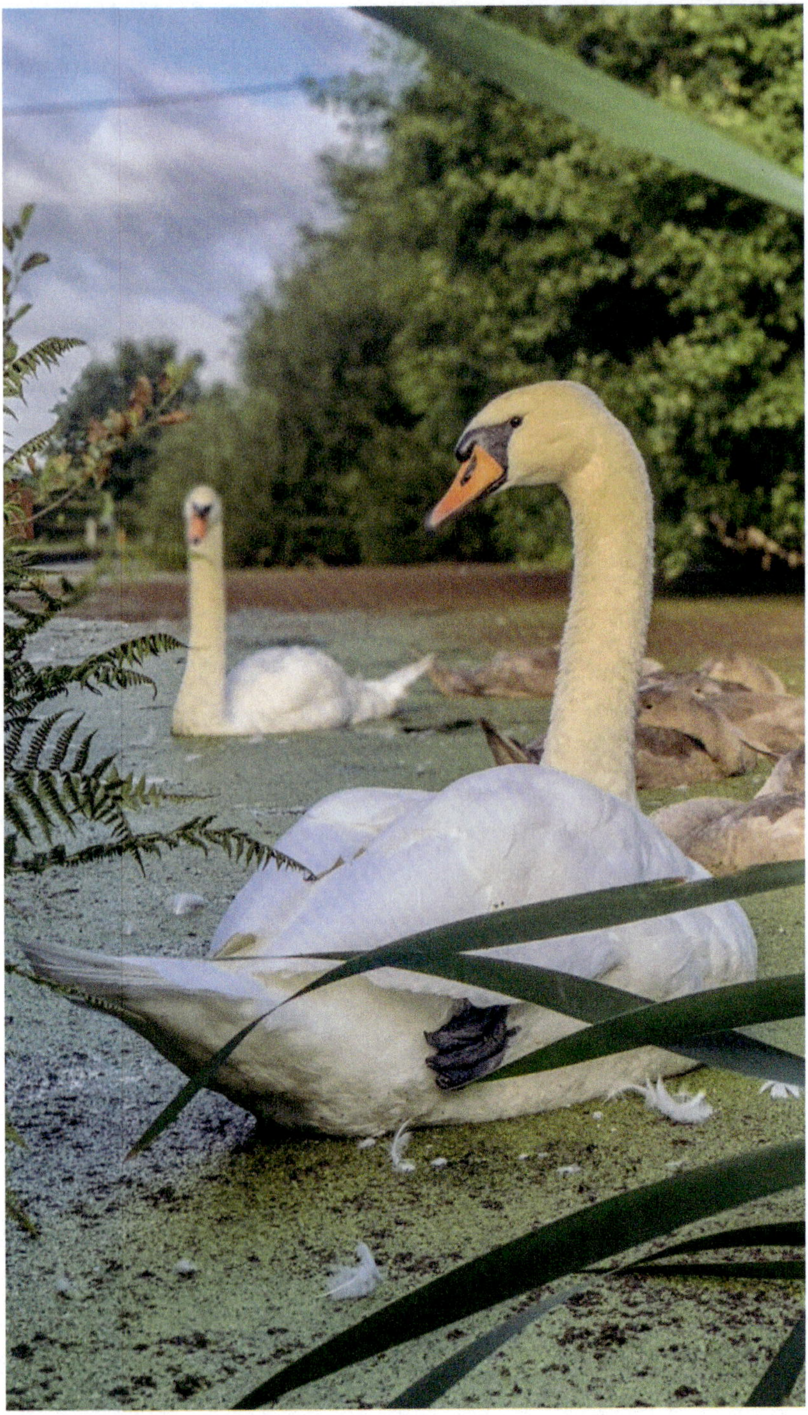

PARENTS

"Parents" portrays a pair of swans residing in close proximity to my location. They stand as vigilant guardians of their offspring on the tranquil canal. In this snapshot, their demeanor exudes a remarkable sense of calm in response to my presence.

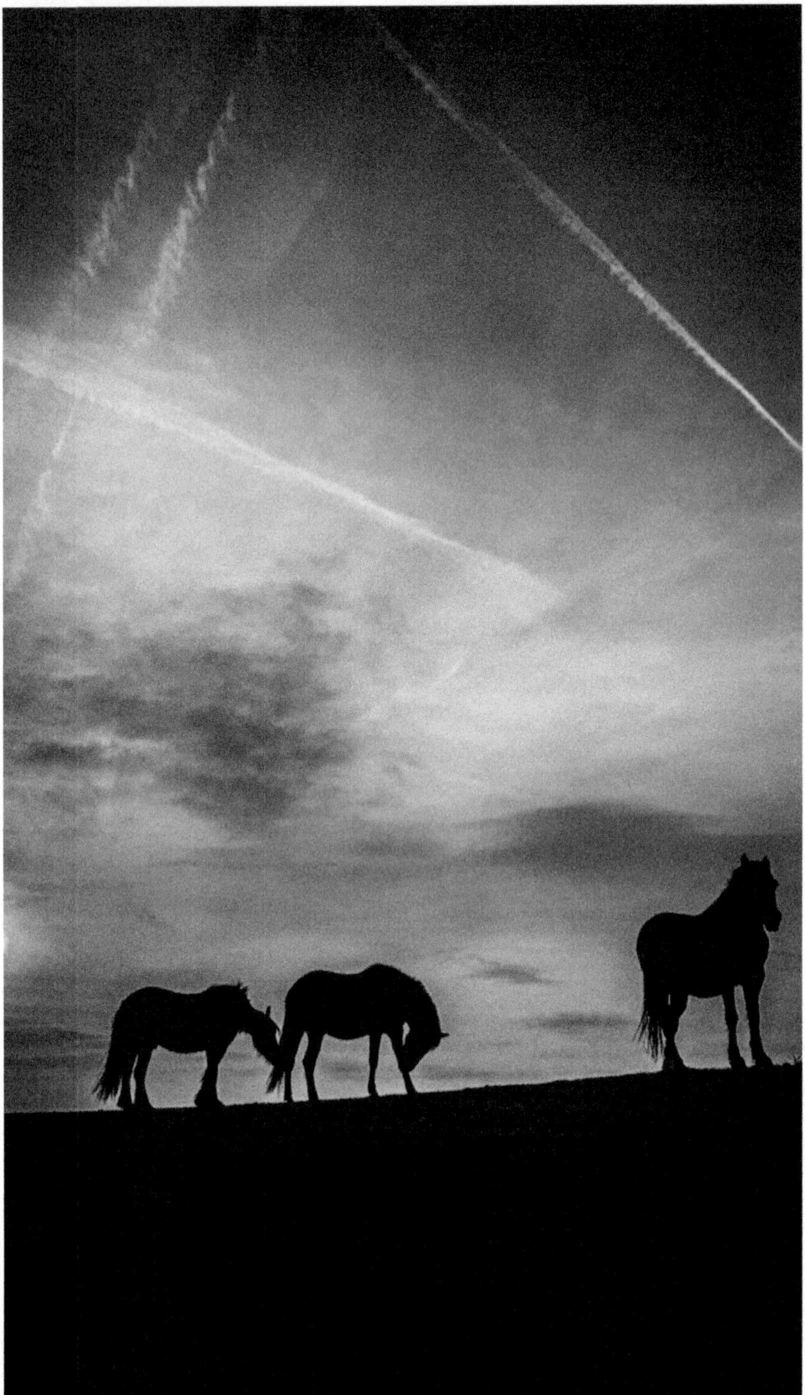

HORIZON

"Horizon" is an image I captured during a tranquil morning in Smithills. The subtle beauty of a winter sunrise served as the backdrop, where three horses formed an exquisite and captivating silhouette. I was compelled to capture the moment instantly.

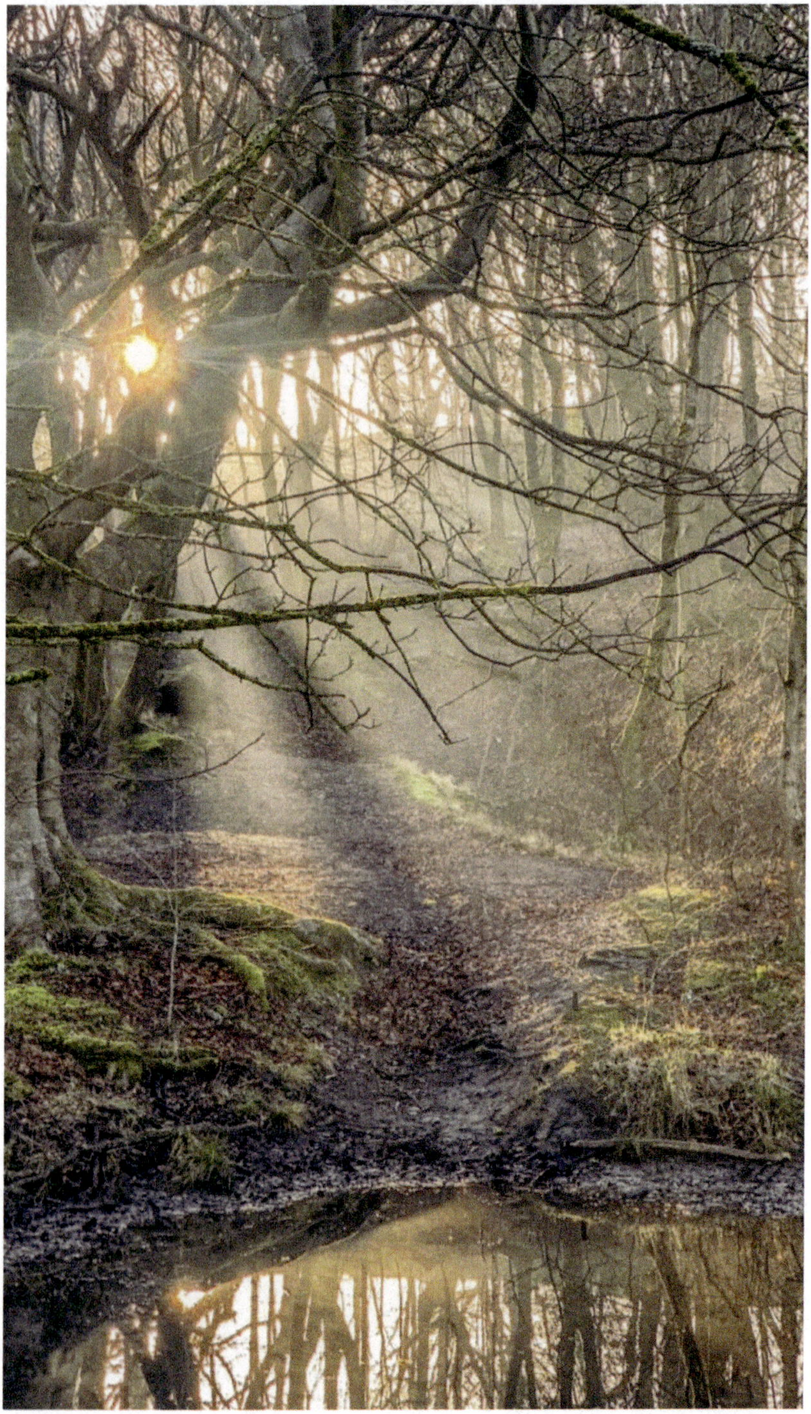

B E A M

"Beam" is the kind of photograph that demands swift capture. A mere minute later, a drifting cloud or the shifting sun would have caused the vibrant beams of sunlight piercing through the trees to vanish, and the moment lost.

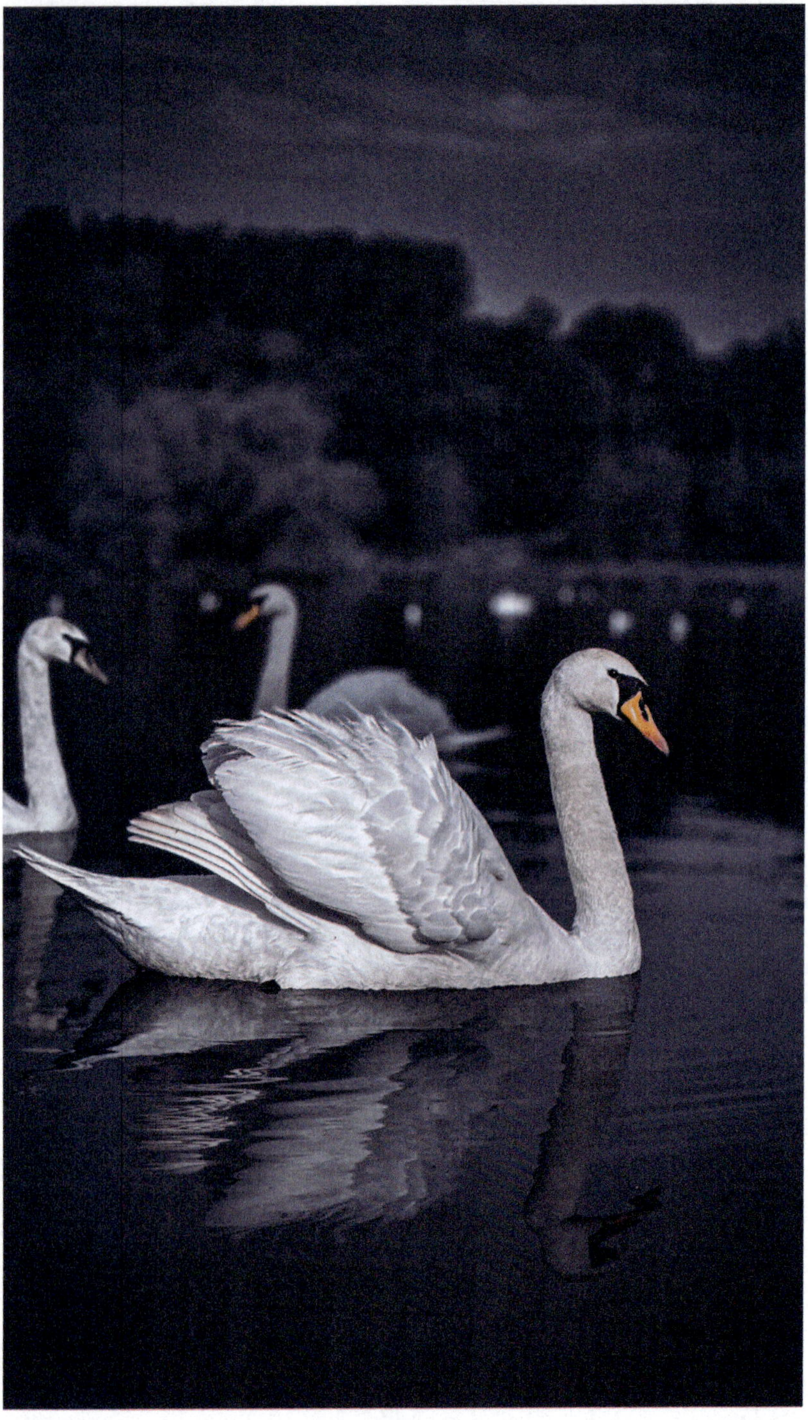

C A L M

"Calm" to me is a tranquil image that soothes whenever I look upon it. Taken in the quiet of morning, when there was no one around. Gradually, the swans approached, curious if I bore any treats, allowing me to seize this serene instant through my lens.

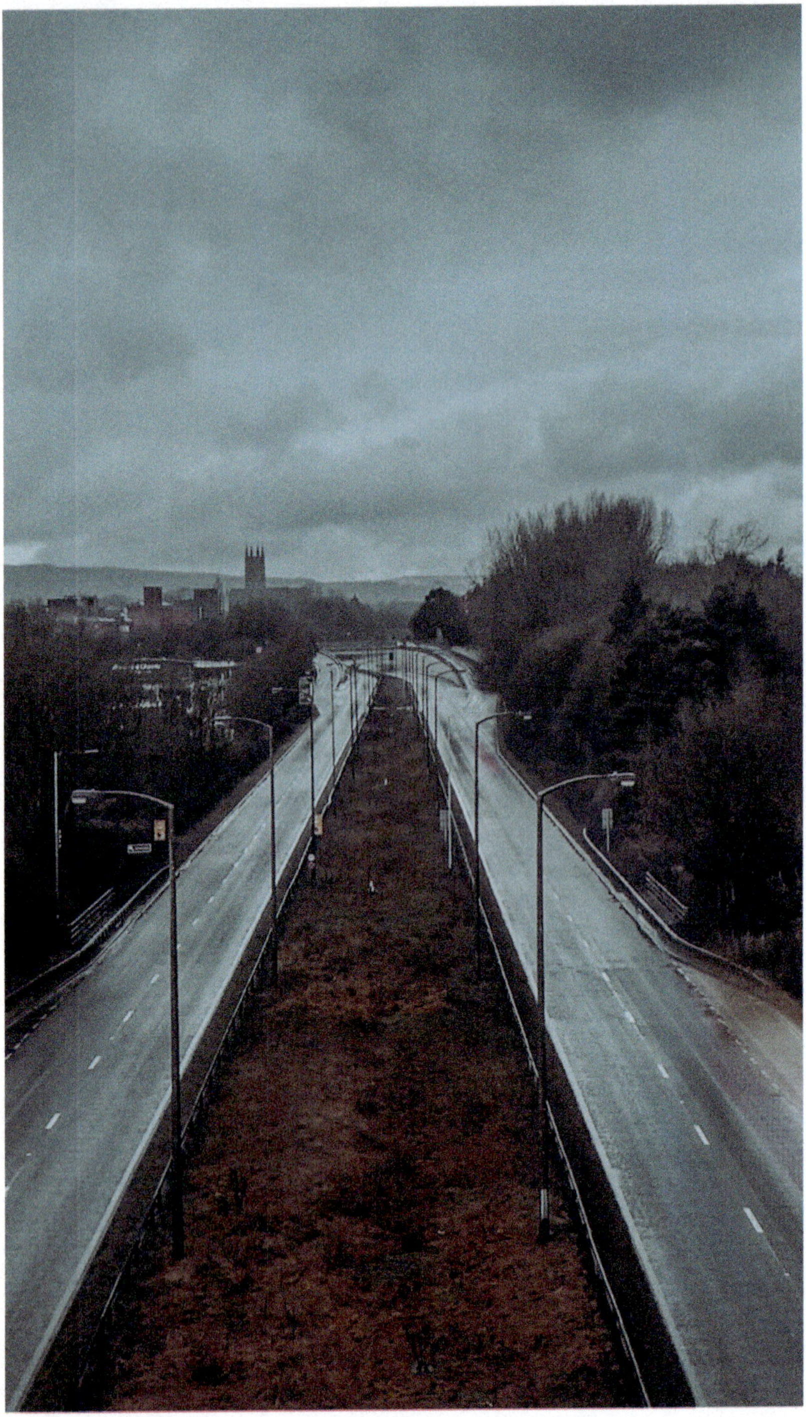

W O R K

"Work" is a photograph captured during the rush-hour morning commute that many undertake. Through a long exposure, the cars vanish from the streets, rendering the scene surprisingly serene amidst the typical hustle and bustle of this busy time of day.

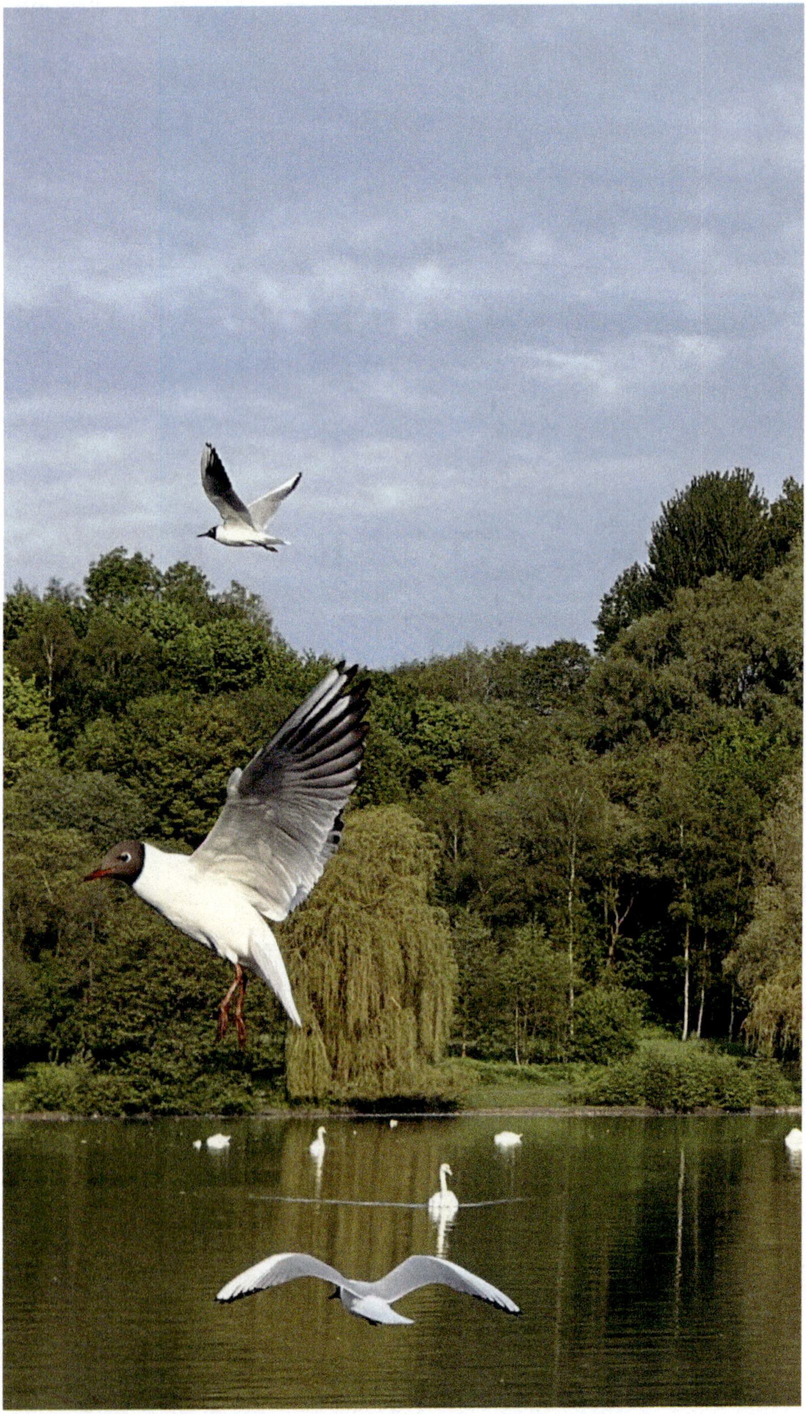

N E W

"New" bears its name as one of the initial images I captured with my new phone. I intentionally visited a nearby bird haven, armed with bird food in my pocket. The seagulls were particularly delighted that morning, and so was I with this shot.

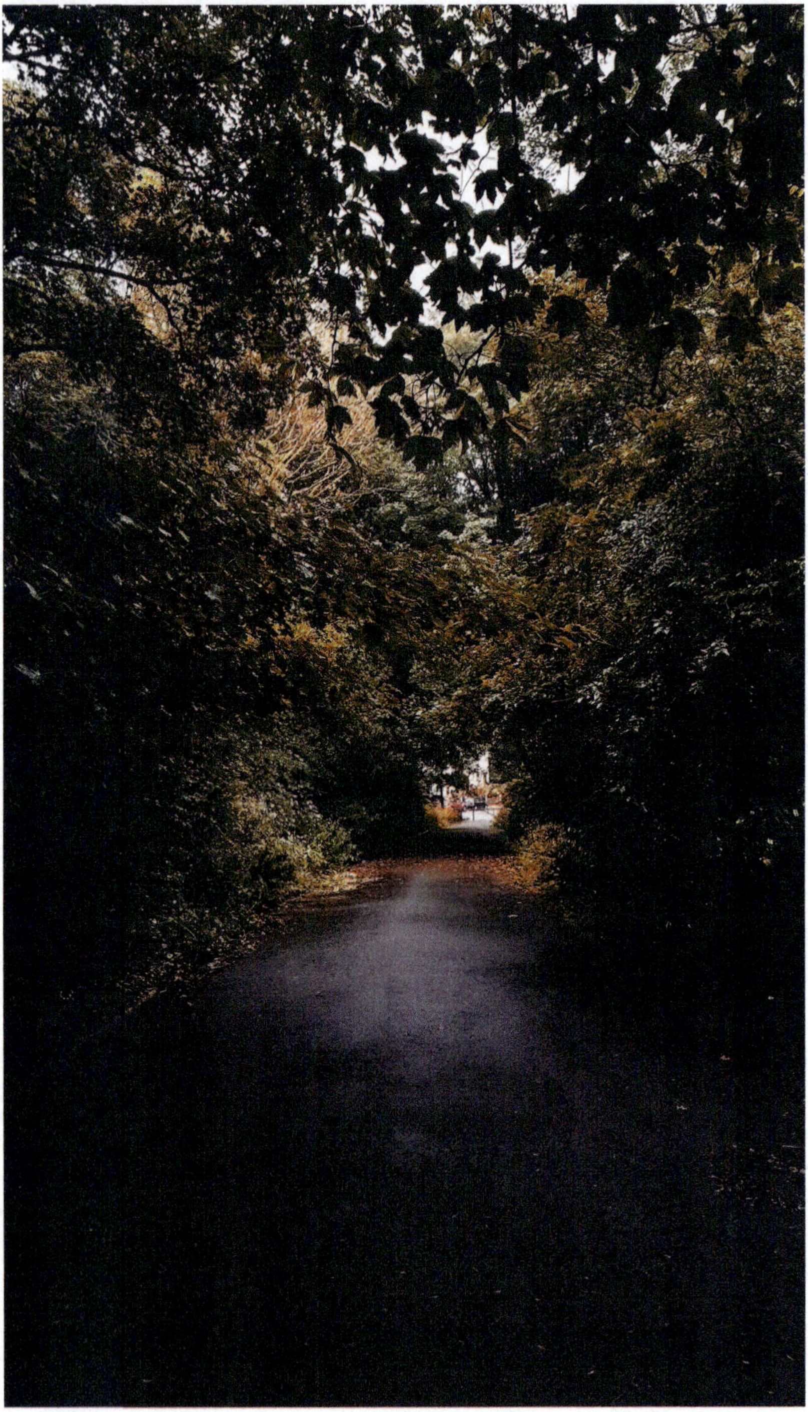

REARVIEW

"Rearview" is a lesson I learned from Howard. Sometimes, our attention is so fixed on the path ahead, causing us to overlook what's behind us and potentially miss out on capturing wonderful moments like this one.

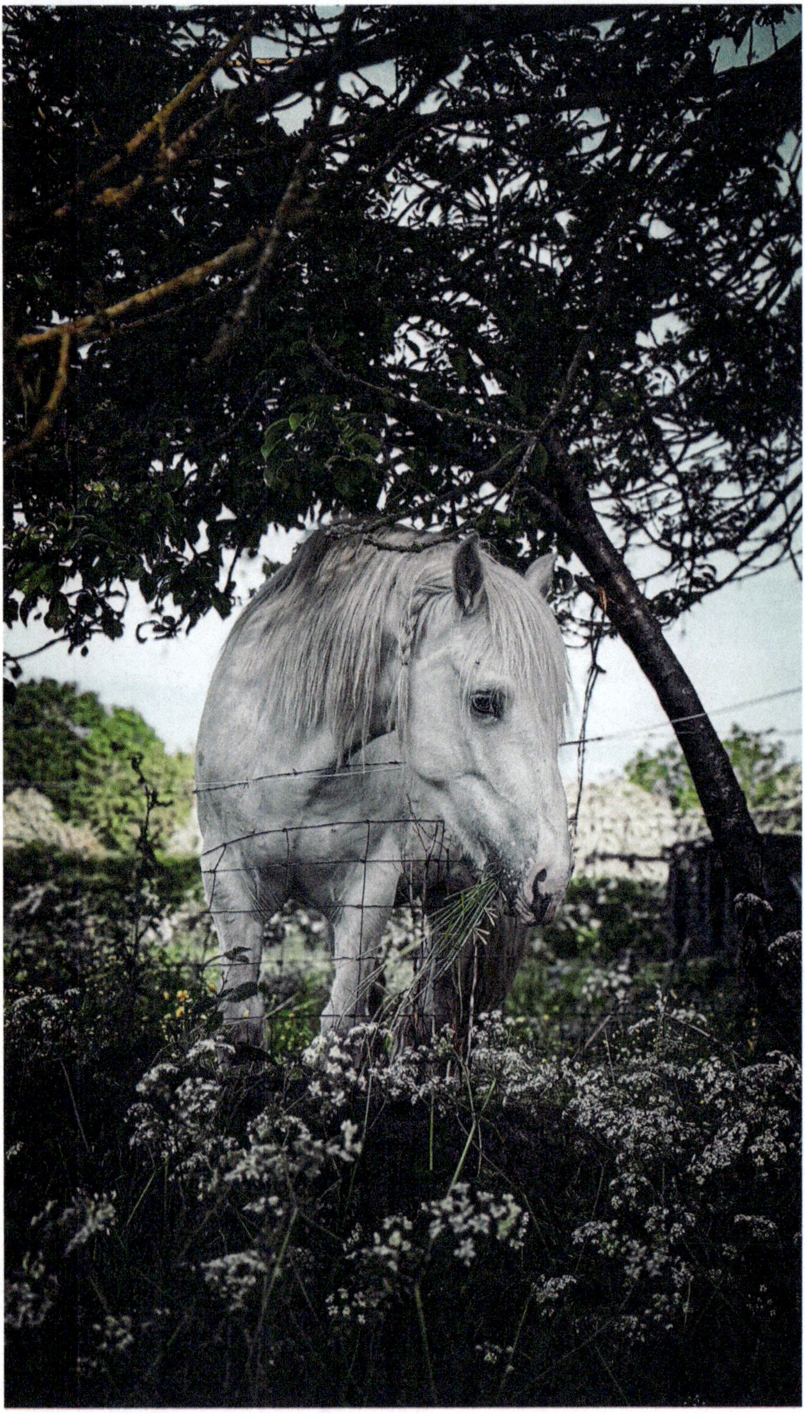

FRIEND

"Friend" is the title, as this horse kindly waited while I dismounted my bike and readied my camera. After the photo, I fetched a bunch of long grass just out of its reach as a treat to say thanks, which it was very happy with, so I took another shot.

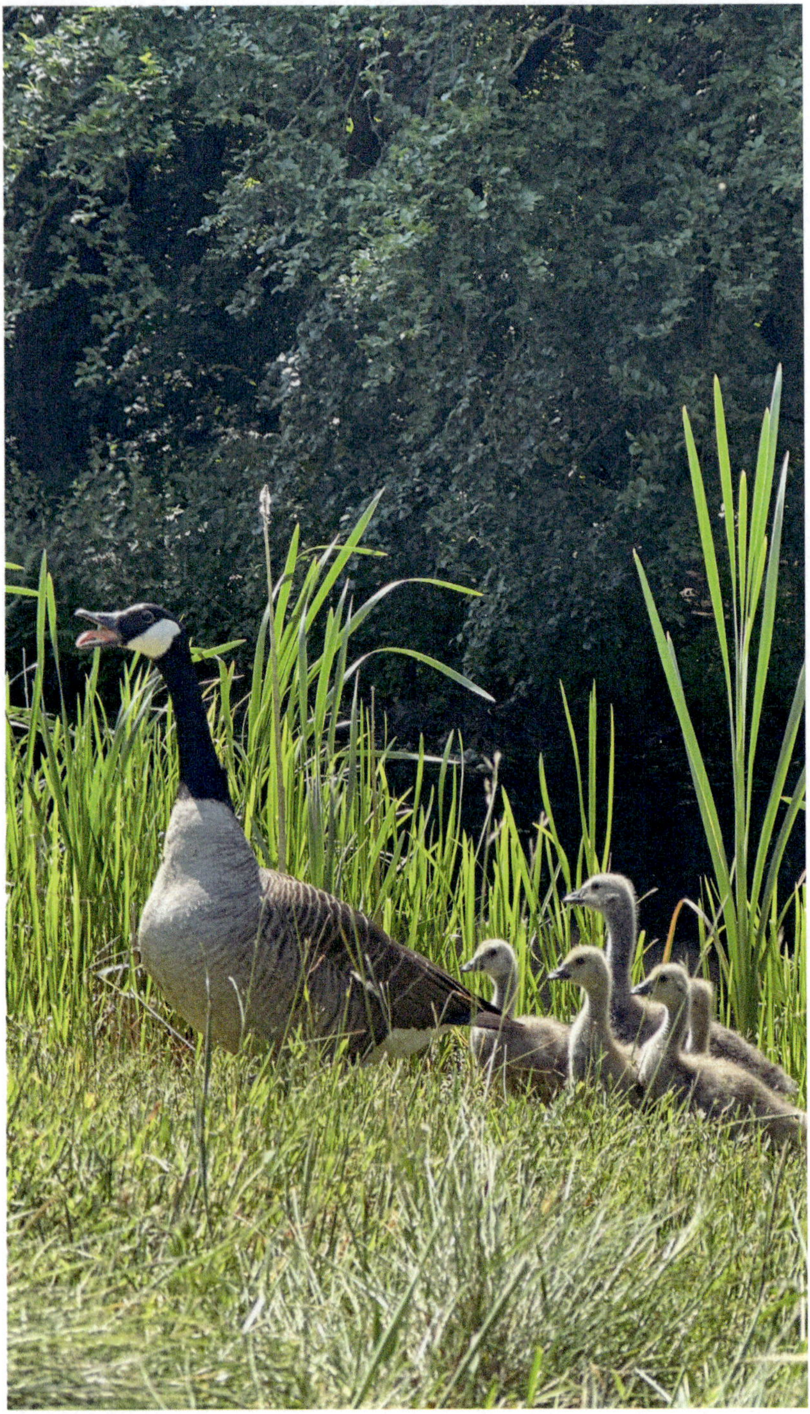

FAMILY

I captured the image "Family" a few weeks after regularly visiting the same stretch of canal around four times a week. During these visits, I fed a goose and its offspring. As time passed, they developed a strong fondness for my presence.

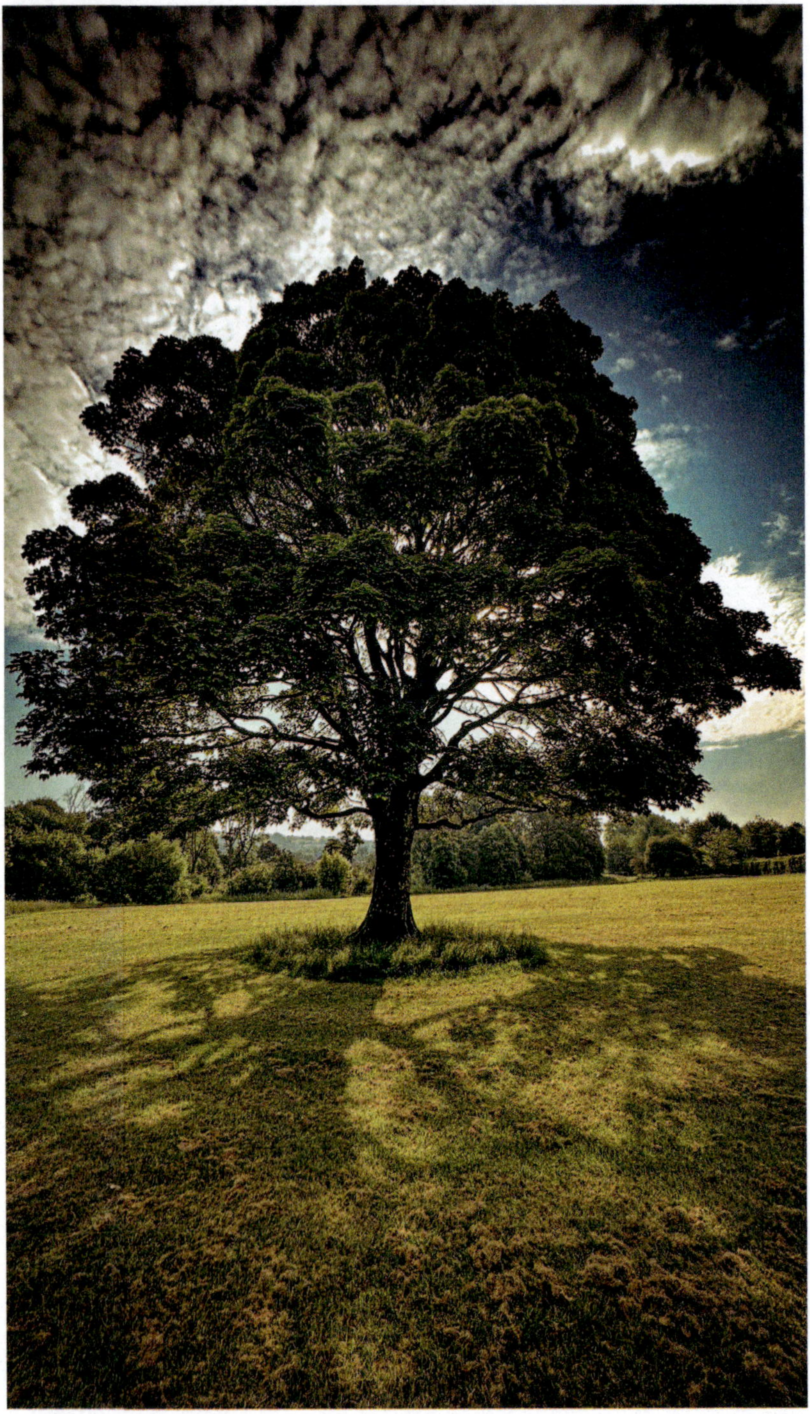

MAJESTIC

I titled the photo "Majestic" because, honestly, why wouldn't you? The image features a magnificent solitary tree, bathed in the glow of a sunrise against a stunning skyline. It's a scene that's hard not to appreciate.

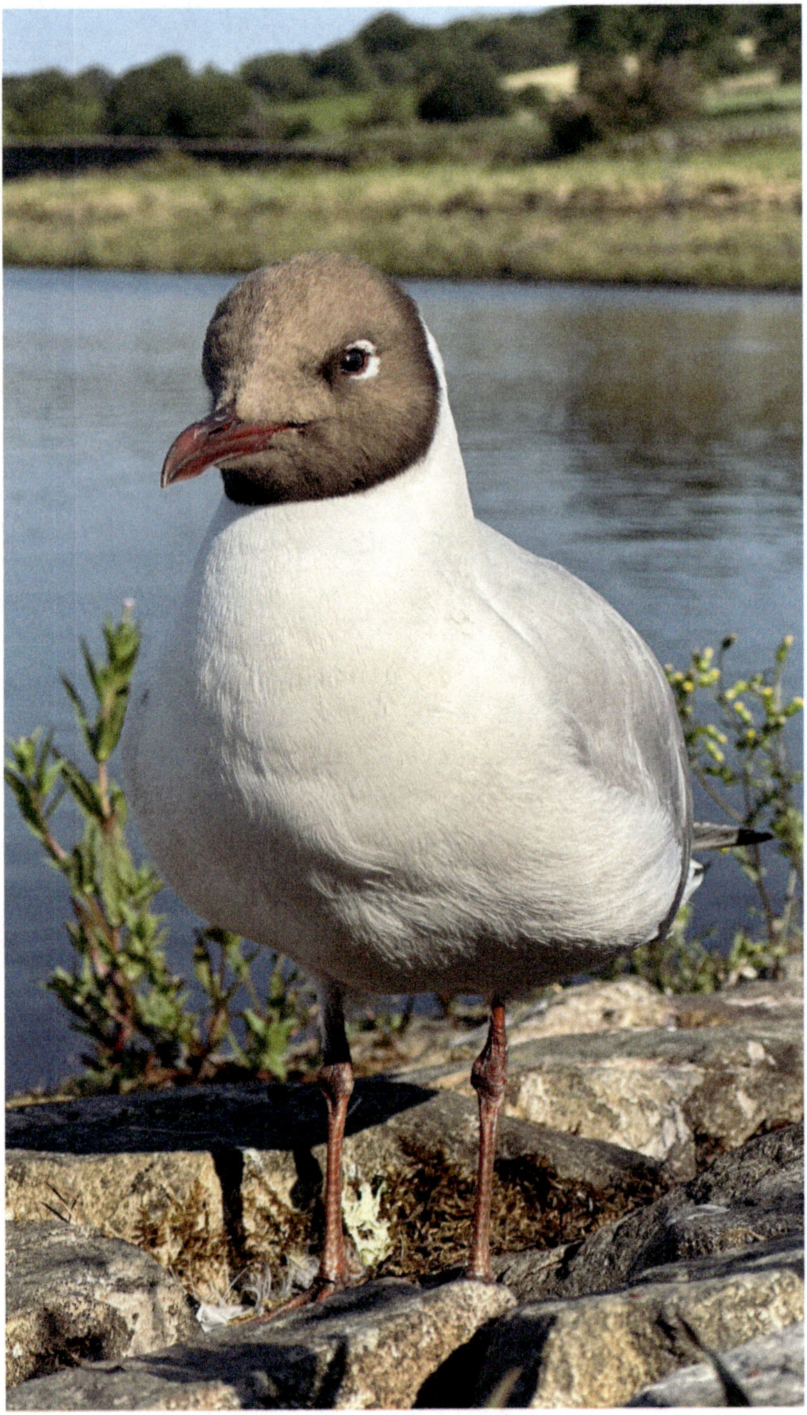

NATURE

"Nature" captures a poignant moment. A gull permitted my dog's close approach, an immediate indication that it wasn't in good health. I snapped a picture, even offering a gentle stroke, before leaving it by the water. This sadly reflects the course of nature.

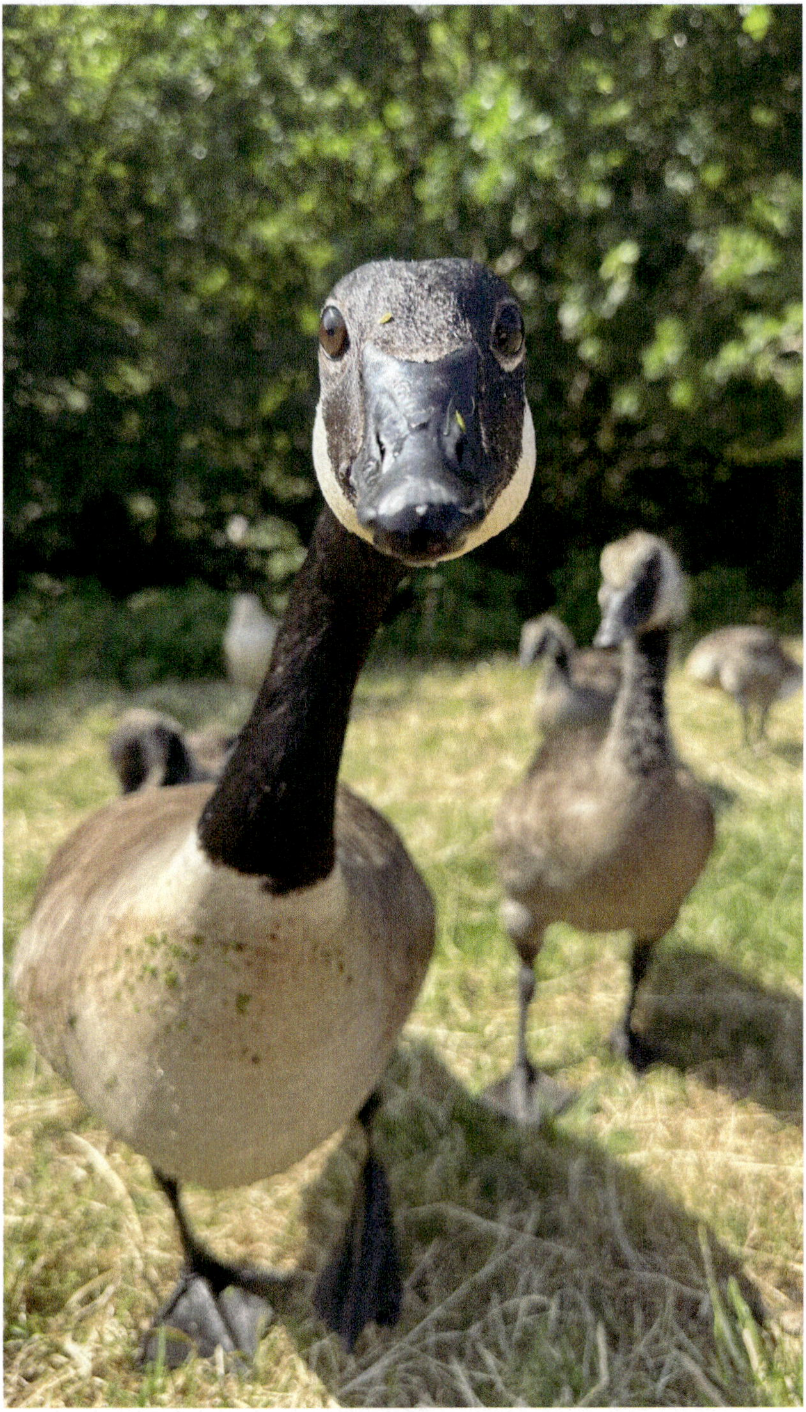

H E L L O

"Hello" is an image that never fails to bring a smile to my face. As I grew acquainted with the goose and its young, they developed a playful boldness, demanding food before posing for photos. Here the goose is impatiently looking for his breakfast.

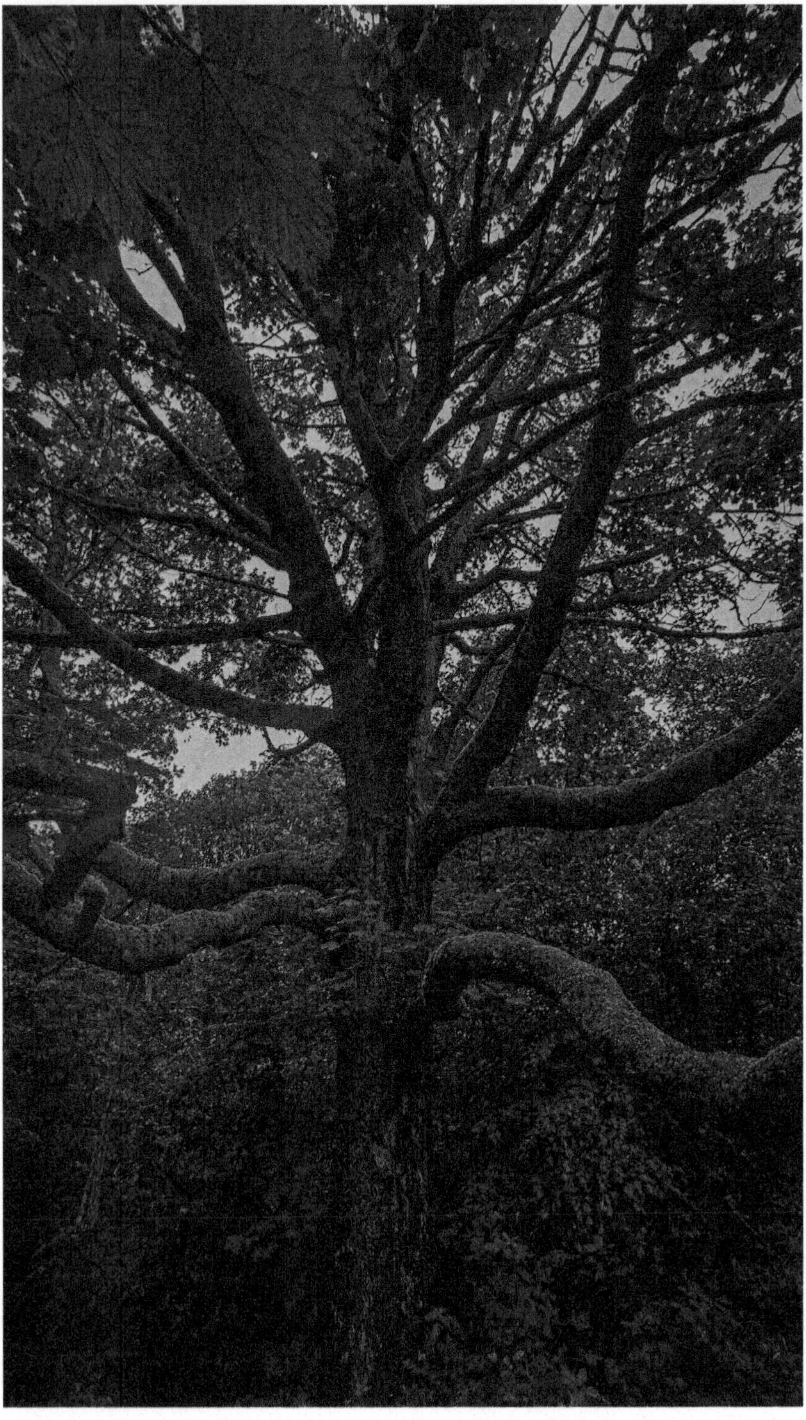

CLIMB

"Climb" is a snapshot I captured of an intriguing tree. Although tree's can be challenging to photograph, its appearance evoked memories of the type of tree that was ideal for climbing as a child, with lots of branches almost spiralling out of control.

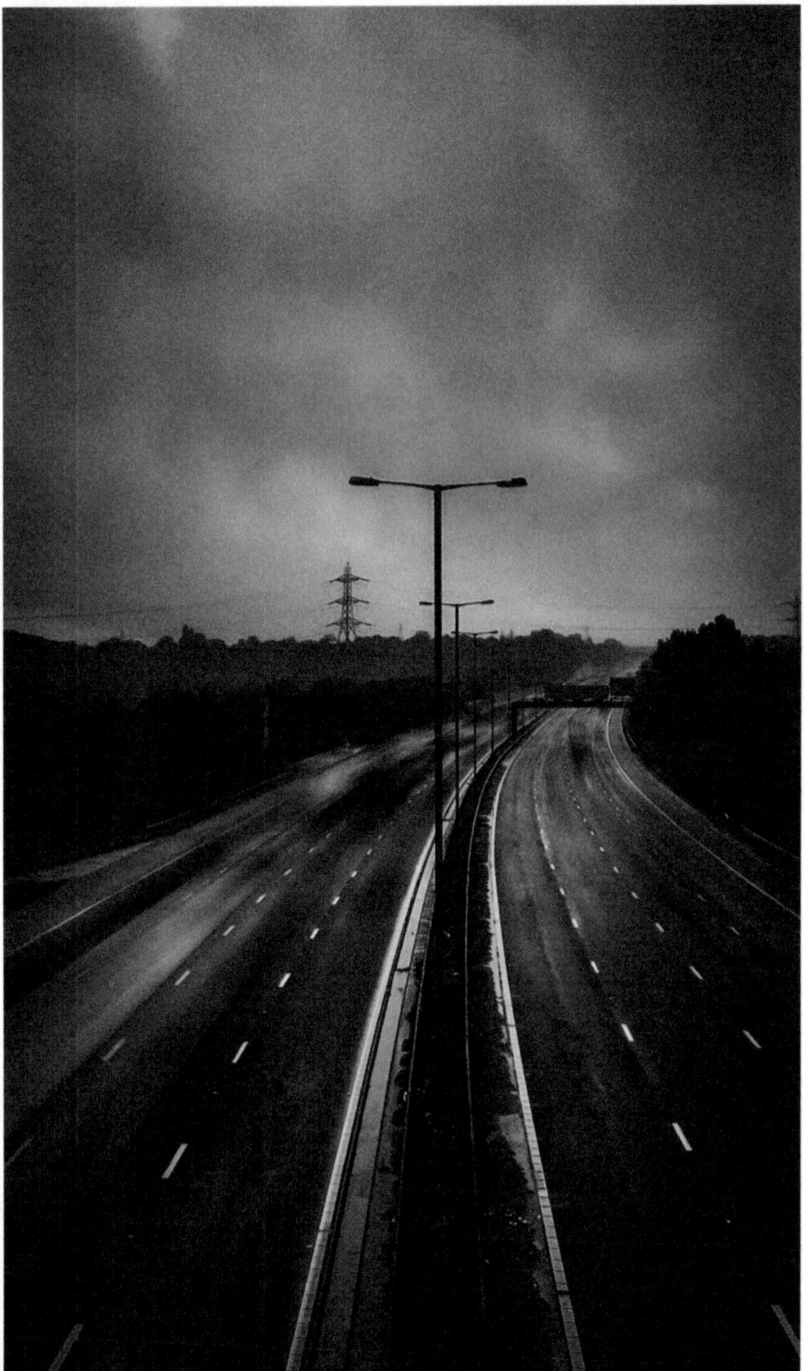

SPEED

I snapped the photo titled "Speed" while walking Mollie over a motorway. In some instances, you have just a fleeting moment to seize a picture. This short window for deliberation can lead to unexpectedly happy outcomes, as was the case here.

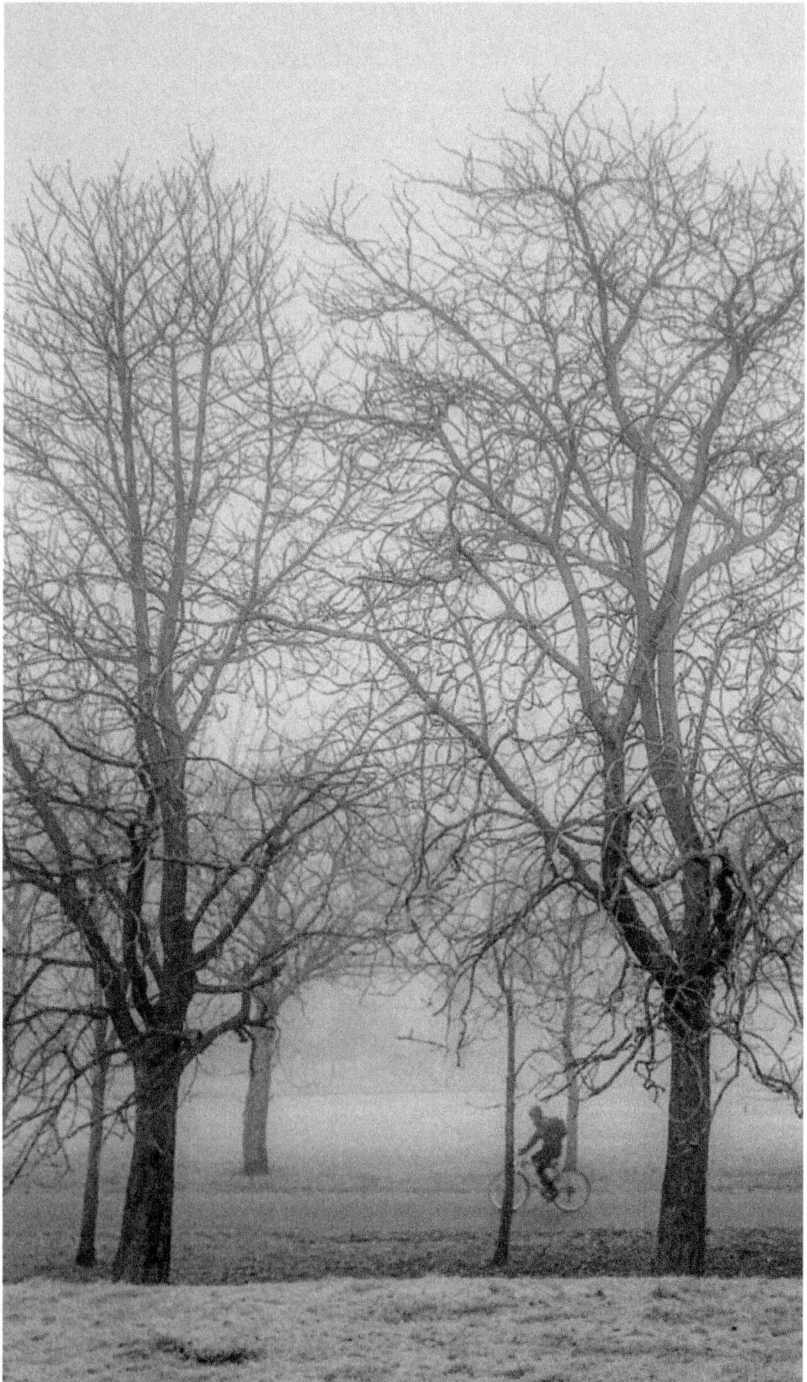

COMMUTE

One chilly winter morning, I captured the photo named "Commute." As a cyclist emerged in the distance, en route to work, I couldn't help but admire their dedication despite the frigid temperatures. I quickly took my gloves off to take this picture.

Coping mechanisms

As the calendar pages turned and the seasons shifted, I began to view life through a new lens, likening it to a theme park. Life, much like a theme park, was filled with its own twists and turns, its ups and downs. There were days when I felt like I was on a high-speed roller coaster, and others when life seemed to move at a gentler pace. But what stood out was the recognition that I held the reins of this theme park – I was in control.

In a theme park, you decide which rides to experience. No one can force you onto a roller coaster; you have the choice to watch from the sidelines if that's what you prefer. This newfound perspective was my revelation. The negativity that often surrounded me – whether it was family arguments, news reports, or discussions of global conflicts – no longer held the power to drag me down without my consent. I realised that I had the autonomy to shape my own experience.

When family disagreements erupted around me, I learned that I could choose to step away, creating my own space of peace. The pervasive negativity of the news, which tended to focus on the darker side of life, could be silenced with a simple press of a button. Engaging in conversations that took a negative turn was also a choice; I could opt to redirect discussions or gracefully exit when they veered into unfavourable territory.

It was about actively deciding what I would let into my world and what I would shield myself from. Just as I had learned to embrace new activities and viewpoints, I was now equipped to navigate the external influences that had once taken a toll on my mental health.

The theme park analogy became a reminder that while life might be unpredictable, my response to it wasn't. It was a gradual shift, but it marked a pivotal change in how I approached challenges and uncertainties. With this mindset, I was better prepared to tackle each day, each twist and turn, on my own terms.

As I delved further into self-improvement and entrepreneurship, armed with a newfound awareness of my mental health, my reading expanded. I revisited the realm of entrepreneurship, a domain I hadn't explored since my twenties. This time, however, I approached it with a fresh perspective, one that prioritised my well-being.

One of the crucial lessons I absorbed was about the insidious nature of negativity – how it infiltrates our lives through various channels, such as the news. I began to recognise that the news, although it might seem like a source of information, often perpetuates the same narratives, just with different characters and figures. War, famine, death, corruption, political turmoil – these were recurring themes that persisted over time. I realised that consuming such content wasn't conducive to maintaining a positive mindset. I unearthed the fact that the news is designed to capture attention, with a particular focus on triggering the amygdala, the part of the brain that's primed to respond to negative stimuli. It's a mechanism that's evolved to prioritise negativity over positivity. Discussions with friends about staying informed by consuming media raised questions. "How do you stay aware of world events if you don't follow the news?" they inquired. Even the thought of the answer felt tinged with negativity.

However, I had come to understand that "everything" is indeed happening in the world. The key was to choose where to focus my attention. I learned that the media unconsciously trains us to think negatively first, with its primary goal being ratings and revenue from advertisers. Beneath the surface, the news isn't a charitable endeavour – it's designed to provoke uncertainty, acting as a hook to keep us perpetually engaged. In a world that seeks certainty, the media exploits our quest for it, rather than truly offering solutions.

The analogy between news and sugar resonated with me. Just as sugar might provide a quick burst of energy but isn't nourishing in the long run, the news might satisfy curiosity momentarily but can contribute to a negative mental state. With these realisations, I made a conscious decision to cut out news consumption from my life. It was a deliberate step toward preserving my mental well-being, shielding myself from the constant influx of negativity that the news delivered.

By letting go of the news, I created a mental space that allowed positivity to flourish. I was no longer bombarded with stories that stirred unease, and I found solace in focusing on the present, my passions, and my growth. In this digital age, where information is readily available, I discovered that being informed wasn't synonymous with being saturated in negativity. It was a powerful realisation that had a transformative impact on my daily life.

Setting yourself up to win

With my renewed focus on self-improvement, I delved into the art of upgrading my circle of friends, or more precisely, identifying and distancing myself from the negative influences. It brought to mind a lesson I had learned back in my mid-twenties, during a part-time night shift job at Asda. I had just left a design agency and found myself in a transitional phase, uncertain about my next steps.

During those shifts, I maintained a low profile, putting in my hours and then heading home. However, a man much older than me struck up conversations, and our chats gradually became a regular occurrence. At that point, I had decided that I wanted to pursue higher education, to bolster my experience with qualifications. It was an exciting decision for me, even if it wasn't the traditional route of attending university first. I eventually decided to confide in my co-worker about my plans.

His response, though, left me disheartened. He dismissed my aspirations with a wave of his hand, telling me it was a waste of time and that I should simply buckle down in my current job to earn money. The enthusiasm that had fuelled my decision was crushed under his negative perspective. In a fit of anger, I lashed out at him, letting him know exactly what I thought of his unsolicited advice.

The following day, my grandma shared some sage advice with me. She suggested that it's often best to keep one's hopes, dreams, aspirations, and plans close to the chest. Why? Because she had observed that most people tend to react to these aspirations with ridicule or negativity, unintentionally dampening the fire of enthusiasm. Her words resonated with me, highlighting the importance of guarding my dreams from those who might inadvertently undermine them. As I reflected on this experience and her advice, it reinforced my understanding of the significance of surrounding myself with individuals who uplift and support my aspirations. I realised that the quality of my relationships significantly impacted my mindset and outlook on life. From that point on, I made a conscious effort to connect with people who shared similar goals or at least showed genuine interest and encouragement in my endeavours.

In the aftermath of my encounter with the negative co-worker and my grandmother's advice, I became more cautious about sharing my aspirations with others. Soon after, I stumbled upon a captivating video online, featuring a speaker whose name now escapes me. However, the message he delivered left a profound impact on me. He elaborated on how, when you choose to pursue something that challenges the conventional norms of those around you, it can threaten their established worldview.

He explained that people often develop a particular perspective on what constitutes a successful life, shaped by their upbringing, societal expectations, and personal experiences. For some, success might be defined by a steady job, a mortgage, raising a family, and acquiring possessions. If you dare to strive for something beyond this familiar narrative, if you challenge yourself to dream of a different path – not necessarily a superior one, just distinct – it can be unsettling for them.

Consider this: your choice to reach for the stars, to explore the unknown, can unnerve those who prefer the safety of the ground. Instead of embracing your aspirations or cheering you on, they may unconsciously pull you down, attempting to maintain the comfort of their own status quo. Their reaction isn't necessarily driven by ill intentions, but rather by the fear that your success would highlight their own complacency. If they can't achieve something, they may instinctively believe that you shouldn't either – and sometimes, they may not want you to succeed because it shines a light on their own lack of effort.

This realisation was a game-changer for me. I recognised that my drive to challenge myself and pursue my dreams were bound to encounter resistance from some quarters. It wasn't a reflection of my abilities or potential; rather, it was a manifestation of other people's insecurities and reluctance to leave their comfort zones. Armed with this understanding, I made a conscious decision to be selective about the individuals with whom I shared my aspirations. I sought out those who were open-minded, supportive and shared a willingness to grow and learn alongside me. This change in approach helped me foster healthier relationships and create an environment where my dreams could thrive without being dampened by undue negativity. Amid my pursuit of entrepreneurship and improved mental health, I came to realise the vital significance of eliminating negative influences from my life. While this might seem like a challenging task for many, I found it relatively manageable due to my inclination toward solitude. I discovered that there were acquaintances within my social circles who had a knack for dwelling on pessimistic topics, and their negativity would often seep into my own mindset. Though it might not have an immediate impact, spending time with such individuals gradually began to weigh me down – sometimes long after our interactions had concluded. In response, I made a conscious decision to distance myself from these negative influences. Now, when I say "remove," I don't mean that I overtly declared my intentions to cut them out of my life. Instead, I opted to avoid their company altogether. If they reached out through texts or invitations, I tactfully responded that I was occupied with other commitments. Over time, the frequency of their messages dwindled, and the connections weakened.

In some cases, this process led to a natural fading of relationships. Certain individuals ceased to be part of my life, while others remained on my Facebook friends list as distant acquaintances. The nature of these connections transformed – from people I might have once engaged in lengthy conversations with, to those I'd simply exchange a polite wave with if our paths crossed. The conversations that used to sap my energy were replaced by the freedom to focus on more uplifting interactions.

This practice was liberating and transformative. By creating a space free from negativity, I experienced a newfound sense of mental clarity and emotional well-being. The decision to remove myself from such draining interactions was instrumental in fostering a healthier mental environment, one that was conducive to personal growth, positivity, and the pursuit of my entrepreneurial dreams.

As time went on, I started to see the effects of focusing on the positive aspects of life and training my brain to spot opportunities. It began with a simple practice of asking myself what truly mattered to me and being specific about my goals. Writing these down and revisiting them regularly became a habit. While the changes weren't immediate, I noticed a shift in my perception over time.

As I continued this practice, I began to notice opportunities around me. It wasn't just about finding extra income, but also about pursuing things I loved and enjoyed. My dog walking business became more than just a way to spend time outdoors; it evolved into a source of income and fulfilment. Conversations about design work led to unexpected freelance projects, and an introduction to a start-up company opened up new avenues for growth.

Depression had once loomed large, threatening to consume my life. But now, positivity was asserting its influence. The more I focused on the positive, the more I realised that it wasn't just about seeking out opportunities; it was about changing the lens through which I viewed the world. The more I trained my mind to see the good, the more the good seemed to find its way to me.

It's important to note that this process wasn't a magical solution. It required consistent effort and a commitment to shifting my mindset. There were still tough days, moments of doubt, and setbacks. However, my newfound approach allowed me to handle these challenges with greater resilience. I learned that positivity wasn't about denying the existence of negativity; it was about choosing to focus on what uplifted and empowered me.

In the journey to overcome depression, I discovered that taking control of my thoughts and perceptions could make a world of difference. I realised that by actively seeking out the positive and training my brain to recognise opportunities, I could gradually reshape my life. This was a process of continuous growth, self-awareness, and conscious choice – one that had a profound impact on my mental well-being and overall outlook on life.

Dealing with panic attacks

Amidst the multitude of resources available to tackle panic attacks, I've discovered that a one-size-fits-all approach rarely fits the bill. This chapter delves into my personalised coping mechanisms, born from the realisation that each panic attack is a unique manifestation. My intention is to shed light on strategies that might resonate with those who, like me, have struggled to find effective methods in the sea of information.

Re-framing panic as misplaced excitement has been a revelation. It's remarkable how closely these two emotional states align in terms of physical symptoms: the pounding heart, constricted chest, and clammy palms. Recognising this parallel, I've employed the tactic of searching for reasons to be excited when panic strikes. I mentally sift through upcoming events, projects, or even mundane experiences that might spark a sense of anticipation. By linking one of these sources of excitement to the panic, I've managed to redirect my mental focus, lessening the intensity of the attack and sometimes even transforming it into genuine enthusiasm.

The second method I used was time. Time can feel like an eternity during a panic attack, as minutes stretch like hours in the grip of anxiety. To counter this temporal distortion, I've adopted the practice of meticulous timekeeping. The act of noting the onset of an attack and recording its duration serves as a lifeline. As I flip my attention from the chaos within to the passing seconds on my watch, a profound transformation often takes place. Observing that panic, like rain clouds, eventually passes, offers a comforting reassurance. Additionally, realising that my experiences echo the time lines of others who share similar struggles brings solace. Tracking time during panic attacks can be surprisingly helpful. Try making a note when you feel an attack coming on and when it starts to subside. Many people experience panic for similar durations, like around an hour. Knowing how long you might have to endure the discomfort can actually make it feel less overwhelming. This practice gives you a sense of control and a reminder that panic is temporary. It's also reassuring to realise that others share similar time lines for their panic experiences. The simple act of observing time passing can be like a lifeline during the chaos of panic.

Another method I used was talking. Reaching out to someone, whether through a phone call or face-to-face interaction, proved to be an unexpected yet effective strategy in my battle against panic attacks. However, the key was not discussing the turmoil I was experiencing or receiving calming advice. Instead, engaging in casual conversation about any topic unrelated to my anxiety became a lifeline. The power of distraction emerged as a potent tool, redirecting my mind away from the overwhelming sensations and thoughts that accompany panic. As I engaged in conversation a subtle transformation unfolded. The simple act of actively listening and responding to their words shifted my mental focus. It was as if the very act of speaking and listening wove a protective barrier against the storm, providing me a temporary respite from the panic.

The fourth method I used was laughter. Humour emerged as an unexpected ally in the midst of panic attacks, though not infallible. Its discovery was serendipitous, providing relief on occasions when anxiety felt overwhelming, highlighting its unpredictable impact on individual responses. Recalling funny memories or turning to sources like Netflix's stand-up comedies acted as catalysts.

Lastly, when panic hits, a technique that has been a game-changer for me: paying attention to my surroundings. It's all about focusing on what I can see, hear, and feel in the moment. I take a mental inventory of colours, textures, temperatures, and sounds around me. By doing this, my mind shifts away from the panic and gets anchored in the present. It's like telling a story in my head, describing what's happening around me. This helps me create a kind of safe zone where the panic starts to lose its grip. It's more than just a distraction – it's like connecting with the here and now.

Social media

I want to take a moment to talk about addiction, and it's important to realise that the word "addicted" isn't limited to drugs. There's a whole world of addictive behaviours out there, some of which can be just as harmful. When we hear "addiction," we often think of substances, but there's more to the story. I've already mentioned how the news can get a grip on us, pushing us into a cycle of seeking out negative information. But another sneaky addiction is social media. It's a relatively new issue in today's world, one that can trap us in endless hours of scrolling, leading to procrastination, addictive behaviours, and feelings of depression and anxiety.

Let's dig deeper into this topic. Social media isn't just about sharing photos and updates; it's also about how our brains respond to it. When we use social media, our brains release chemicals like oxytocin and dopamine, which make us feel good and connected. Interestingly, these same chemicals are also released when we gamble, smoke, or drink alcohol. The difference is that those activities have age restrictions and support systems in place, while social media is a bit like the Wild West.

Social media is skilled at making everything look picture-perfect, even when it's not. Most people only show the best parts of their lives online, creating a skewed view of reality. Spending hours scrolling through everyone's highlight reels can lead to feelings of inadequacy and sadness. Especially when you're already feeling down, this can make things worse.

One of the smartest choices I made was taking control of my social media experience by utilising mute settings and unfollowing individuals. This doesn't mean cutting ties entirely, but rather curating what appears in my feed. By unfollowing someone, I ensure that their posts no longer clutter my news feed without having to unfriend them. It's a small action that yields a remarkable impact on mental well-being.

Some individuals on social media may not realise the impact of their frequent 'happy posts' on those struggling with depression. While it might not be entirely their obligation to filter their content, it becomes our duty to regulate what we expose ourselves to. There were instances when I found myself experiencing feelings of envy or sadness upon witnessing what seemed like others leading ideal lives. In response, I chose to mute their posts and stories. It wasn't that I begrudged their happiness, but rather, I recognised the need to cultivate my own sense of contentment instead of comparing myself with them.

I discovered that our digital landscape has transformed us into seekers of instant gratification. Think about the inconvenience of suddenly reverting to old-style texting - it's almost unimaginable, considering how accustomed we've become to the speed and efficiency of current communication methods. This culture of rapid interaction has permeated not only our communication but also our interactions with technology and media.

By embracing the power of unfollowing, I discovered two things. First, it's a testament to our innate human tendencies, illustrating how our digital behaviours mirror our desire for speed and ease. Second, it brings to light the quality of the connections we have on social media. It becomes clear that the people I unfollowed were individuals whose updates didn't significantly enrich my online experience anyway. This exercise serves as a reminder that our online networks should comprise those who genuinely enhance our lives and contribute positively to our well-being.

The next step I took was a deliberate examination of who I was following outside of my friends and acquaintances. I set my sights on business accounts, gauging whether I was engaging with sources that nurtured positivity and encouragement. The reality was a bit stark. Instead of inspiring content, my feed was populated with news accounts, conspiracy theories, and sources that fuelled confrontational debates. Recognising the impact this had on my mental well-being, I made a conscious decision to cleanse my virtual environment. The unfollow button became my tool of choice. I severed ties with accounts that were feeding negativity into my feed. The news accounts that seemed to amplify my anxieties, the conspiracy theories that only served to stir unease – they were gone. In their place, I embraced a new stream of content. Creative accounts, those filled with art, inspiration, and entrepreneurial insights, found their way onto my feed. This intentional shift ensured that when I turned to social media in moments of low spirits, I wasn't subjecting myself to a barrage of negativity.

This process wasn't just about unfollowing; it was about choosing what I allowed into my mental space. The accounts I followed now mirrored my desire for positivity, creativity, and personal growth. Scrolling through my feed became an act of nourishment rather than a source of stress.

The process of making these changes opened my eyes to the essence of healing as a dynamic journey of experimentation and learning. It dawned on me that my generation, the Millennials, often possesses an inherent impatience due to growing up in a world defined by instant gratification. A world where desires can be fulfilled with a simple click and where waiting is virtually non-existent. Need something? Amazon delivers it overnight. Want to connect? A text replaces a letter. The movie you crave? Stream it immediately. Even dating is a mere swipe away. This paradigm of immediate satisfaction has subtly ingrained itself in our expectations.

Ironically, we find ourselves impatient when it comes to our own well-being. We seek quick fixes for complex emotional challenges, yearning for immediate solutions. This realisation hit me: we've become captives of instant gratification, yet we're often intolerant when it comes to our mental health journey. It's as if we've forgotten that life, unlike the digital realm, lacks an app for instant transformation. I came to understand that embracing change, especially in the realm of mental well-being, requires a fundamental shift in perspective. It calls for patience, acceptance, and a willingness to tread a path of trial and error.

Some things I have learnt

Upgrading your friends: Our friends play a big role in where life takes us. Hang out with gamblers, and you might become one too. Spend time with heavy drinkers, and you could end up with a drinking problem. The idea of upgrading your friends, often suggested by motivational speakers, isn't just about finding buddies you like. It's more about cutting ties with people who don't share your goals. You won't find new friends until you let go of the old ones. If you want to change your life, you've got to change too. Think about it: the people you're around can influence you a lot. If you're with folks who are into certain things, you'll likely get into them too. This applies to positive or negative stuff. The advice to "upgrade" your friends isn't only about finding new pals who fit better. It's about ditching the ones who aren't on the same page as you. It's like making room for new things by clearing out the old.

Making changes can be tough, but it's what leads to growth. If you're after a different life, it starts with you. It's like they say, "If you want things to change, you've got to make changes." Remember, the path you take isn't just about your choices; it's also shaped by who's walking with you. Your friends are like pieces of a puzzle that form your life's picture. They shape your thoughts, decisions, and where you end up. Your life's story is woven together by the influence of those you spend time with. So, when you look at your friends, know that they're not just friends – they're part of your journey and what lies ahead.

Blaming parents: Pointing fingers at our parents for the twists and turns of our lives might seem like an easy out, but it's a path that leads to a dead end. Early on, I realised how many folks would lay blame on their parents for various aspects of their journey or simply badmouth them. Amidst this, a paradox emerged – complaints flowed about mothers being distant, yet others would grumble about being smothered by constant advice and support, driving them to their wit's end.

As conversations continued, more gripes surfaced. Some lamented their modest backgrounds, taking jabs at their friends who'd grown up with more privileges. Yet, paradoxically, those from wealthier families would voice their own frustrations about feeling overly pampered, lacking the skills to manage without relying on their parents' resources. What became evident was that the cycle of complaints was a never-ending loop, unaffected by the circumstances.

It's true, we can't choose our parents. We inherit the family we're born into, with all its quirks, imperfections, and idiosyncrasies. But herein lies the truth – if you scrutinise closely, many of those who blame their parents would likely still find something to complain about, even if circumstances were reversed. It's a cycle that perpetuates itself, unswayed by the changes in circumstances. There comes a juncture when the echoes of blame need to be silenced. A moment to acknowledge that while our parents play a significant role in shaping us, we have the agency to define our paths. Our lives are not solely an outcome of our parents' actions; they're a culmination of our choices, mindset, and determination. Adulthood beckons us to stand on our own two feet, to take ownership of our decisions, and to recognise that the narrative of our lives is ultimately a story we craft.

In this quest for self-reliance, it's pivotal to shed the mantle of parental blame. Our parents did what they thought was best with the resources and knowledge they had. Now it's our turn to navigate our way, embracing the challenges and opportunities that come our way. Blaming our parents is an evasion of responsibility, a mere distraction from the transformative journey that awaits when we take the reins of our lives into our own hands.

Change your life overnight: You can drastically change your life any day you want, what stops most of us is fear of the unknown. Changing your life might seem like a far-off goal, but here's the truth: You have the power to kick-start that change any day, whether it's tomorrow or even right now. All you need to do is take that first step.

Think of it like building a path with bricks. Each choice you make adds another brick, gradually shaping the path you walk. The big secret? It's not about grand gestures; it's the everyday actions that count.

Starting is the key. Whether it's adopting a new habit, tweaking your diet, exercising regularly, cutting off negative friendships, or making a bold career move — these choices can redefine your life. And don't buy into the idea that life-changing moments only happen out of the blue. You're not just a spectator; you're in charge of your journey.

Transformation doesn't mean you have to reinvent yourself completely. It could be as simple as getting up a bit earlier, opting for healthier food, or reading different kinds of books. These small shifts, done consistently, can lead to big changes over time.

Remember, transforming your life is all about making choices. Each day presents an opportunity for change. The idea that change only comes unexpectedly is a myth. You have the power to drive change on your own terms. Every choice, every action is like adding a brick to your path. So, as you embark on this journey of transformation, embrace your ability to shape your story. It's about taking steps, making choices, and building a life that reflects your aspirations and dreams.

Undeserving Mindsets: It's remarkable how many of us are unwittingly entangled in the web of thinking that we're unworthy of financial freedom. While I've touched on how the news can shackle us in a cycle of negativity, now let's turn our gaze toward television and money. Take a moment to ponder: How many daytime TV shows revolve around the prospect of winning money? If you're like me, you can probably list six without much effort. Yet, the prize pools on these shows rarely exceed a couple of thousand pounds. As the sun sets, the trend continues – with another five evening shows I can conjure on the spot. And this is merely scratching the surface.

Venturing beyond game shows, we find competitions tucked into the fabric of other programmes – be it the news on certain channels, sporting events, or various segments offering prizes ranging from £50k to a shiny new car. And then, there's the omnipresent lottery, a beacon of hope for many. But why does all of this matter? This brings us to a more profound observation: we're subtly conditioned to harbour a subconscious belief that we're only deserving of money if we win it through luck or chance. These constant reminders of money as a prize rather than an earned reward can erode our sense of self-worth. The quiet murmur of doubt creeps in – a whisper that perhaps we're not deserving of financial abundance unless fate smiles upon us.

So, why raise this point? Because our belief in our own worth is at the core of it all. When you truly start to embrace the idea that you are deserving of abundance, regardless of how it manifests, your life takes a seismic shift. Embracing your inherent worthiness sets off a chain reaction. It reshapes your thoughts, influences your decisions, and transforms your actions.

In the realm of financial wellness, this shift in perspective becomes a catalyst for change. Suddenly, you're empowered to seek opportunities, negotiate for better compensation, and invest in your skills and knowledge. The script of life flips from waiting for a chance to actively pursuing opportunities. The dormant potential awakens, and you begin to pave a path that leads to prosperity. Unravelling the conditioned belief that you're only deserving of money through chance is a pivotal step toward financial liberation. Recognise that the value you bring to the world transcends the whims of luck. Embrace the understanding that your inherent worthiness is not tethered to a lottery ticket or a game show victory. As you embody this truth, you unlock the door to transforming your financial reality. With your worth as the cornerstone, you embark on a journey that leads to a life defined by abundance, purpose, and the boundless potential that resides within you.

Living in the Moment, Breaking Overthinking: If you're like me and tend to overthink, switching off can be a real challenge. But I learned something that made a big difference – being present. When I'm working, I focused on the work, not on how I haven't seen my family or need a break. And the same goes for the other side – when I'm on vacation or hanging out with friends, I don't let my mind wander to work. Setting boundaries is key. I set specific times for work and rest, and I'm present in both. It's a simple thing, but it changed a lot for me. It's about being in the moment, wherever you are, without getting pulled into thoughts about what you should be doing somewhere else. This approach helped me find a balance that I never had before.

Having routines helps too. I know when it's time for work and when it's time for downtime. This way, I can focus on what's in front of me without distractions. It's the same when I'm taking a break – knowing that it's my time to recharge without worrying about work.

This practice is far from fancy, but it had a big impact. Being present in each moment brought a sense of peace. It's about shutting off the tug-of-war between what you're doing and what you feel you should be doing. Not being present leads to dissatisfaction, a loop of frustration we create for ourselves.

Figuring out how to stop overthinking and be in the moment is powerful. It takes some effort to stay focused where you are, but it's worth it. This simple change makes you appreciate work and downtime more. By letting go of distractions, you stop being stuck in your head. Remember, contentment is about being where you are, not getting lost in the past or worrying about the future. As you practice this, you'll discover that the secret to feeling fulfilled is embracing the present.

When you're at work, be at work, when you're at home be at home.

Wishing for better times: Human nature often leads us to wish for things rather than putting in the effort to attain them. This tendency brought to mind a scene from the movie "Bruce Almighty," where Morgan Freeman's character, portraying God, poses a thought-provoking question: "If someone prays for patience, you think God gives them patience? Or does he give them the opportunity to be patient? If he prayed for courage, does God give him courage, or does he give him opportunities to be courageous?"

This notion struck a chord with me and resonated deeply. It prompted me to shift my perspective on wishing and desiring. Instead of merely wishing for fewer problems or challenges, it became clear that the true path lay in wishing for, and actively cultivating, the skills needed to navigate and conquer these challenges. In a world of quick fixes and instant gratification, we often fall into the trap of seeking an escape from our problems rather than tackling them head-on. This realisation led me to recognise the power of transformation through action. Wishing for fewer problems was, indeed, an exercise in futility. Instead, the focus should be on developing the skills and abilities required to address and resolve these problems effectively. The analogy presented in the film highlighted the role of opportunities in granting us the very attributes we seek. Patience, courage, resilience – these virtues aren't bestowed upon us in a neatly wrapped package. Instead, they emerge as we engage with the challenges life presents, seizing each obstacle as an opportunity to cultivate and display these qualities. Incorporating this perspective into my life, I began to shift my wishes from mere desires for an easier journey to fervent hopes for the growth and development of skills that would equip me to navigate even the most complex terrains. The act of working on these skills emerged as a meaningful endeavour, propelling me toward personal growth and transformation.

Embracing the Art of Self-Preservation: It's a common human tendency to resort to moaning and grumbling, replaying the same complaints like a broken record. This observation became glaringly apparent as I noticed that even close family members and friends were often caught in a loop, revisiting the same issues time and again. They would lament their problems with an uncanny repetition, articulating the same arguments as if they were on a continuous loop.

Initially, I found myself exasperated by this pattern. I sincerely wanted to help, offering countless suggestions on how they could break free from this cycle of endless complaints. Yet, despite my well-intentioned advice, every time I encountered them, they'd embark on the same lamentation journey once more. It was a frustrating cycle that left me feeling drained and helpless.

Over time, however, a shift in my perspective began to take shape. I realised that some individuals are not yet ready to embrace change or seek solutions, even if those solutions are right in front of them. It dawned on me that, at times, people must be willing to help themselves. It became increasingly clear that my continuous engagement in their cycle of complaints was not only affecting my well-being but also enabling their persistent behaviour.

This realisation led me to embrace what I termed the "art of being selfish." It wasn't about becoming self-absorbed or uncaring, but rather about prioritising my own mental health and emotional well-being. I recognised that I had a responsibility to protect myself from the negative energy that accompanied their constant complaints and unwillingness to heed advice.

This shift involved setting boundaries. When someone approached me with complaints, I candidly expressed that I didn't want to be part of that conversation. If they sought to criticise or gossip about others, I respectfully declined to engage. This newfound sense of self-preservation allowed me to shield my mental space from the incessant negativity. This process of self-prioritisation was a revelation. It illuminated the fact that, despite my best intentions and well-thought-out advice, some individuals are steadfast in their commitment to complaining without seeking resolutions. It taught me that while I can offer guidance, the choice to change ultimately rests with them.

Learning to protect my mental well-being by embracing a degree of selfishness was a transformative lesson. It unveiled the truth that, no matter how much wisdom and advice you offer, some individuals will remain entrenched in their patterns of negativity. This lesson affirmed the importance of setting boundaries to safeguard my own mental health.

Friends come and go: Friendships aren't constant. Leaving a job many years ago, I thought coworkers would be lifelong friends, but they faded away fairly quickly. I've learned bonds aren't just about time together, but reconnecting effortlessly. Those we truly value stick around, reciprocating effort. Like Mark, a friend who has offered years of guidance, lent a compassionate ear, and instilled the importance of reciprocity. Maintaining our bond requires mutual commitment; just as he checks in on me, I make it a point to do the same for him. A simple message like 'Life's been hectic, but you're on my mind, and our catch-up is overdue' carries tremendous weight.

Friendship's dance isn't about time; it's about sincere connection. Mark's taught me bonds need shared effort. Whether advice, listening, or a heartfelt message, nurturing connections defines true friendship.

Closing

If you've journeyed through this book, my hope is that my message has resonated and found a place within your thoughts. I'm just an ordinary person, someone who, like many, has faced certain disadvantages but also enjoyed numerous advantages. Central to my growth has been the art of framing life's narrative. The question arose: Does life simply happen to us, or is it unfolding for us? This shift in perspective has been pivotal, driving me to unearth the reasons behind events, fostering a personal evolution that has yielded profound results. Comparing my life to others offers a perspective-altering journey. I've learned that life's canvas, whether painted with hardship or fortune, is malleable to interpretation. Framing circumstances as opportunities for growth, regardless of their nature, has catalysed transformation. The more I embrace this mindset, the more I find myself evolving into a better version of myself - more skilled, resilient, confident, and the list goes on.

This revelation also uncovered a truth about the nature of mindset. It's akin to a lens that filters our perception of the world. When we believe life is happening to us, that everything is steeped in negativity, we become attuned to spotting unfavourable occurrences. Negativity can be likened to a contagious ailment that infiltrates our being, influencing our emotions, thoughts, and actions. The dark spiral that negativity can induce often leads to the shadows of depression and anxiety.

However, there is a way to break free from this cycle. It lies in the transformation of mindset. The realisation that we have the power to shift our lens and re-frame events is transformative. By doing so, we alter the trajectory of our emotions and decisions. The cloud of negativity dissipates, making way for positive opportunities that may have otherwise remained hidden.

I've lived through the consequences of harbouring negativity, of bottling up emotions and refraining from seeking support. When the storm finally erupted, I found myself ill-equipped to navigate it. The importance of developing a robust mindset became evident. It's a mental armour that shields us from the storms of life, granting us the strength to face challenges head-on.

As we wrap up this chapter, my message is clear: shaping our mindset is a powerful tool in our journey. It's about recognising that life, with all its intricacies, is a canvas we can paint with intention. It's understanding that how we perceive events shapes our reality. By adopting a mindset of growth, resilience, and positivity, we harness the ability to thrive even in the face of adversity.

This isn't a tale of going from rags to riches. I still have my moments of low days, occasional panic attacks, and those days when the allure of indulging in a chocolate binge while endlessly scrolling on my phone seems tempting. Yet, and this is the pivotal aspect, the knowledge I've gained has led me to experience fewer of those difficult days than before. Moreover, I now possess the tools to manage them, preventing them from spiralling into something uncontrollable. It's important to note that I'm not claiming to have an infallible solution. Challenges still arise, but my changed perspective and acquired insights enable me to tackle them more effectively. The frequency of such days has decreased, and I've honed my ability to keep them from gaining too much power over me. While my methods might not resonate with everyone, I urge you to discover what does work for you. Experiment, try different approaches, and if one doesn't yield the desired outcome, see it not as a failure, but as a step closer to finding what will work. Each attempt brings you nearer to discovering the strategies that align with your unique needs and circumstances. Embrace this journey of self-discovery and personal growth – it's a process that ultimately empowers you to craft a happier, more fulfilling life.

In closing, I extend my heartfelt wishes for your mental health journey. Remember, no one should bear the burden of suffering in isolation. Your path is important, and I sincerely hope the road ahead is marked with progress and healing. Thank you for taking the time to read my book. Your engagement means the world to me.

Acknowledgements

At this moment, I wish to extend my heartfelt appreciation to a select few individuals whose support has been the cornerstone of my journey in crafting this book. Foremost, I want to express my gratitude to my mother, whose unwavering dedication and tireless encouragement have been a beacon of strength throughout this endeavour. Her commitment to my aspirations goes beyond measure, and I am profoundly grateful for her presence in my life.

Equally deserving of recognition is my grandmother, who has graciously tolerated my incessant requests for her time and attention. Patiently, she listened to the evolving chapters, offering her insights and perspective, and contributing to the shaping of this work. Her willingness to engage and her enduring patience have played a significant role in bringing this book to fruition.

I am immensely grateful to Mark, a true beacon of wisdom and guidance in my journey. His invaluable teachings have illuminated my path in entrepreneurship, molded my mindset, and fueled my motivation. Mark's unwavering presence as a friend who consistently checks in has been a source of inspiration and a testament to the enduring power of genuine connections.

I wish to extend my gratitude to the remarkable individuals who dedicate their time and energy to assisting those grappling with mental health challenges. You are the unsung heroes who shine a light in the darkest corners of people's lives. Your unwavering commitment and compassion make a profound difference, and your efforts resonate as a testament to the incredible impact of human kindness. Your work isn't just a profession; it's a vocation that uplifts, empowers, and transforms lives, embodying the very essence of heroism

Lastly, I believe it's important to turn my gratitude inward. If you, as a reader, have grasped the essence of this book, then you've also grasped the significance of acknowledging oneself. I would like to extend a sincere thank you to myself for embarking on this challenging journey. As I navigated the intricate pathways of writing, I encountered obstacles and triumphs alike. Through it all, I recognised the value of celebrating every little victory and embracing the process of growth and creation.

Writing this book has indeed posed its fair share of challenges. Yet, rather than viewing these challenges as roadblocks, I chose to see them as opportunities for growth and learning. This endeavour has not only expanded my horizons but also allowed me to relish the multifaceted journey it entails.

Feel free to follow me on instagram

◉ @jasongholmes